GHETTO BY THE SEA

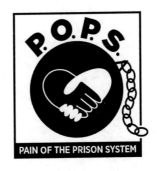

P.O.P.S. THE CLUB
AN ANTHOLOGY OF
STORIES, POEMS AND ART

P.O.P.S.

PAIN OF THE PRISON SYSTEM

© Eduardo Hernandez

Contents

How We Live

Where We Stand

When We Dream

What We Eat

Life at POPS

Life in Reverse

Why We're Here

Friends of POPS

Introduction

This introduction will be short and sweet, because the heart and soul of GHETTO BY THE SEA belongs to the writers and artists you will meet in these pages.

In RUNAWAY THOUGHTS, our first POPS anthology, published in 2014, we regaled readers with the story of how POPS came to be and what we have learned in our years of teaching and from working with teenagers and young adults who have been changed by the pain of the prison system.

In his introduction last year, Dennis explained that the way to inspire teenagers to dig deep and to be brave enough to reveal their innermost feelings and share their core stories is this: Stop talking and listen. Amy wrote about why and how we created POPS as a place for those who have endured the pain and isolation, the sorrow and stigma of prison to find friendship, community, comradeship, compassion, healing, and most of all a place that celebrates all they have to say.

That's all you need to know—except that we also urge you to read every page, including the Acknowledgments, where we've taken the opportunity to offer thanks to those who make this work possible.

Dennis Danziger & Amy Friedman
Co-Founders, POPStheclub.com, Inc.
www.popstheclub.com

Acknowledgments

To our extraordinary volunteers who show up week after week to help inspire us all, and who always shut up and listen: Stacey Cohan, Melanie Keedle, Hannah Schatzle, Anastasia Stanecki, and Madge Stein Woods.

Thank you, from the bottom of our bellies, to the weekly feasts provided by Factors Famous Deli, Superba Food + Bread, Le Pain Quotidien, and Panera Bread. They feed us as if we were royalty.

We were privileged to welcome a number of powerful speakers this year, people who touched our hearts and changed our lives. Gratitude abounds to California's inspector general, Robert Barton; Scott Budnick of the Anti-Recidivism Coalition; teaching artists Antonio Sacre, Alicia Sedwick, and Susan Treadwell; powerhouse speaker and teaching artist Khanisha Foster; prison rights activists Franky Carrillo, Bruce Lisker, Obie Anthony, and Lakeisha Burton; Kelley Whitis of Linda's Voice; writers Christina McDowell and Luis J. Rodriguez, poet laureate of Los Angeles; and artist Phil America.

We are indebted to those journalists who have helped to spread the story of POPS—stories that so inspired Conley-Caraballo High School in Hayward, California, that they recently introduced a POPS club to their own school—the second in the nation. Soon you'll be reading their stories too.

To the justice editor of the Good Men Project, Wilhelm Cortez, who every week features one of our students' stories; to *Education Week*'s Sarah D. Sparks for her remarkable insights into the toll incarceration takes on children and her generous words about POPS; to Lisa Niver for introducing POPS to the readers of *The Jewish Journal*; to *California Educator*'s Sherry Posnick-Goodwin's beautiful article on the way one teacher—in this case our own Dennis Danziger—can change lives; to Diane Lefer for her brilliant work on the impact of incarceration on children; to Madeleine Brand and Christian Bordal of NPR's *Press Play* for their terrific radio story on POPS the Club; and to Boston Woodard for his many stories about POPS (originally for *The San Quentin News* and now featured in his new book; and thanks to Boston for coining the phrase "I was a POPS kid before there was a POPS."

To John Oliver for his deeply insightful rant on America's love affair with prison on his show, *Last Week Tonight*.

To Beyond Baroque for providing a beautiful stage and setting for our students' performance of their work, to Carlye Archibeque for making the show possible, and to Jim Fleck for all the technical help.

To Sens Musiq and his band, Poetic Rhythm, for the music that soothed and enlightened us that day onstage at Beyond Baroque.

To Amy Wakeland and Mayor Garcetti, who invited eight of our students to join some of L.A.'s women leaders for lunch in honor of Rosa Parks Day at Getty House, the mayor's abode.

To Carol Burton for inviting two of our POPS students, Angel De La Cruz and Bianca Lopez, to participate on a panel at the Long Beach Conference for Children with Incarcerated Parents: Trauma, Toxic Stress, and Protections.

To Amy Cheney and the librarians for the In the Margins Award for honoring our first anthology, RUNAWAY THOUGHTS, as one of the top 35 books for the underserved.

To Lauren Marks, our social-media guru, wise and generous editor, and to Kate Zentall, proofreader extraordinaire.

To Reina Roberts for her design genius, and to teachers Chris Wright, Jenna Hughes, Tory Toyama, Hazel Kight Witham, Art Lindauer, and Matthew Cannella for your ever-lasting support.

To Hollye Dexter for generously donating a portion of the proceeds of the sale of her memoir, *Fire Season*, to POPS the Club.

To the Venice High Booster Club for their generosity to Dennis Danziger and Chris Wright for helping to produce this volume.

To Jamie Masada of the Laugh Factory, and to Tim Allen, Lowell Sanders, and Frazer Smith for a night of comedy, with all proceeds going to POPS the Club.

To Amy's brilliant mentor Rachel Davenport, who is teaching her how to be an executive director in conjunction with the Wells Fargo Executive Director's Leadership Training Institute, and to the indomitable Janets—McIntyre and Schulman. And with gratitude to colleagues Arrowyn Ambrose, Ange-Marie Hancock, and Bill Thompson for their insights and inspiration.

To University of Southern California's Dr. Raphael Bostic and Danielle Williams, for their intelligence and devotion to making it possible to collect data on how POPS impacts students.

To Spoon Jackson, California's Inspector General Robert Barton, Amy Cheney, Boston Woodard, and Judith Tannenbaum who give, and give, and give.

To our stalwart and passionate board of directors: Lydia Flora Barlow, Carol Burton, Stacey Cohan, Dennis Danziger, Anastasia Stanecki, Heidi Tuffias, and Madge Stein Woods, for everything you do to help POPS flourish.

To the Venice High School administration for opening your hearts and doors and being brave enough to say yes. And to Rene Bell-Harbour and Renata Ocampo of LAUSD for your ongoing interest. And to Ramon Camacho and Eric Barron of Conley-Caraballo High School for welcoming POPS the Club into your wonderful school.

And to our generous donors … without whom there would be no books, no feasts, no website, no POPS the Club. Thank you from the bottom of our hearts.

"You can't help it. An artist's duty, as far as I'm concerned, is to reflect the times."

—Nina Simone

© Eduardo Hernandez

Where We're From

Ghetto by the Sea

by De'Jon K. Jones

I come from paradise on one street to the 'hood on the next.
I come from not staying out too late, 'cause that's playing with your life.
I come from being an athlete by day and a gang member by night.
I come from where if you make it to see age 18, you've hit a milestone in life.
I come from where guns are an accessory to your outfit.
I come from where sirens and helicopters are normal in life.
I come from where if you ain't got it, you got to go get it, by any means.
I come from where 90% of us don't have a father figure, and 100% of our
 mothers worry about if we'll make it back home once we step out of the house.
I come from being harassed by police for being on the good side of Lincoln
 Boulevard, the east side.
I come from where if the police interrogate us, we forget how to speak English.
I come from where we push Venice ShoLine Deuce Gang Crip, that's VSLC 2x
 and we rep either 5th, 6th, or 7th Ave.
I am from Venice, CA, 90Z0091, the Ghetto by the Sea.

Portrait of De'Jon K. Jones, © Hannah Schatzle

Walk in My Shoes

by Bianca Lopez

You don't understand till you walk in my shoes. All you see is a happy young girl who hides her problems with a huge smile on her face. But darkness is behind that wonderful smile. She's someone who sees the world as a fairytale but knows in reality it's just a broken glass!

Whenever I hang out with friends, at some point they begin to talk about their brothers. They talk about how those brothers take them places, buy them the things brothers buy their sisters. Their talk makes me feel empty and embarrassed because if they ask me, "Hey Bianca, what does your brother do?" Or "Do you have a brother?" what can I say? That I have a brother, but he is in prison? That I haven't seen him in six years, and no he hasn't taken me places or bought me things? But I don't say that because I sometimes feel that others judge me for having a brother in prison. So I don't say anything much about him.

I want the sister-and-brother bonding and brotherly advice. I want to have a brother I can run to when I have boy problems or other situations that I can't tell anyone else about. I've always dreamt that my brother would be by my side, standing on those bleachers as I walk that Class of 2015 stage. But the thing is, that will not happen because I won't be seeing him for another 23 years.

What hurts most is that every time I see my little sister, Daisy, I picture his face, and I always fear that she will become just like him and follow his mistakes, step by step. She mistreats my parents and even her own sisters. I feel that she doesn't want to be part of our family and would rather spend time with her friends, listen to them instead of her family. She leaves the house without even telling us where she is heading. Those are the little things that my brother started doing—listening to what his stupid friends wanted him to do.

I watch my mom sitting there, her tears pouring, and I think: What did she do to deserve this? Why do her kids always end up chasing the wrong path?

I don't blame my brother for his mistakes, but I'm disappointed in him for not even being here. I see his friends roaming around our neighborhood like they have no cares in the world. They are killing and threatening and manipulating people, and meanwhile my brother is in prison for 29 years for being a witness of an attempted murder. It seems so unfair. One of his friends was accused of kidnapping and robbery and they only gave him 12 years. My brother never pulled a trigger against anyone—there's proof of that. But the detective didn't like my brother and decided not to show that evidence. The first lawyer made Jordan sign some paperwork saying he was guilty. Who would do something like that to a family?

Jordan's friends don't care what we go through. They never come to us or offer money to help him. All they know how to do is to bring violence and mistrust to our family.

I come from a place where jealousy and betrayal exists, where if anything happens, the cops are involved. I come from a place where I'm scared even to walk outside because you never know what will happen between Corning and Hervey Streets. My brother's friends don't care who they hurt—all they care about is getting what they want.

So I have something to tell you. Don't ever tell me that I know nothing about the gang life, the prison system, or not having a brother, because trust me, you won't understand my life until you walk in my shoes.

© Eduardo Hernandez

The Struggle

by Kemontae Dafney

I come from where the odds are against me.

People think Venice, California, is a nice place to visit or live, but not for us African-Americans.

I grew up in Venice and it's always been rough.

Where I live, baseball hats don't represent the major-league teams. If you walk past the wrong street wearing the wrong hat, you're guaranteed to get shot at. In my neighborhood homicides and home invasion robberies happen almost every day.

It's a struggle where I come from, where everybody is trying to find a way to make it to the top. Where you're either in the streets or working in the industries. Where I grew up, you are either a ballplayer or you're on the block banging and selling nickel rocks.

Sadly, many people who were good at sports chose the streets.

In my neighborhood you have to be inside your house before the streetlights come on, and if you aren't you're playing with your life.

I come from a place where people try to make it out, but can't seem to find the right path.

Hispamericana Exquisite

by Elia Guadalupe Espinosa

I am blood of my blood and food of all cultures.

I was never a Hispamericana, a Hispanic and American combined. I was born in the dangerous city of Netzahualcoyotl, Mexico. Brought to America by needs. I grew up like most kids in poverty. My family isn't rich, but we had a rooftop and food on the table. But the beauty of it all was the food. From a savory dish of traditional mole to the finger-licking *molotes* Mother made. It was the food that brought me closer to my culture every day.

Most teens grow accustomed to a different lifestyle. I was brought to Los Angeles, California, when I was five, and I've been here ever since. But I despise change. I hated the language, the people, the school, the city itself, but one thing I didn't hate was the food. Two double cheeseburgers, a side of salted French fries with a strawberry soda is the American dream. I realized in every corner there was not only an American restaurant but also a Hispanic restaurant. America had accepted a little bit of my culture, and soon enough I had accepted a little bit of America.

I am a Hispanic by heart and an American by choice. I was born under the red, white, and green, yet I represent the red, white, and blue. I speak fluent English and Spanish, which run through my blood. I savor the beauty of being a born Hispanic becoming a made American. To this day I am both. I eat, I breathe, and I see both the cultures that molded me.

Twenty Feet

by Alberto Hernandez

Most people think growing up in L.A. is easy. You see, I would believe that if I was wealthy, but I didn't grow up in Beverly Hills, Malibu, or Westwood. I grew up in the ghetto in Mid City L.A. by Crenshaw, where every day is a blessing to be alive.

I am a soldier in this cold world. Only God knows what I've been through. Not knowing when you'll take your last breath. I'm traumatized by the violence.

I lie on my bed and look out the window every night. All I hear is people screaming at each other, sirens in the distance, and ghetto birds in the air.

Not so long ago a guy got stabbed. In the corner where I live. I was asleep, and he was screaming, "HELP." I thought it was a dream. I woke up to move my truck the next morning and stepping out my driveway I saw blood. It was not a dream. An African-American guy got stabbed in the stomach a few steps away from my house. I followed the trail of blood and noticed he walked 20 feet after getting shanked.

That's as far as he went. All along the sidewalk there were puddles of blood. The guy made it all the way to the back of my F-150 truck. Blood covered the tailgate and fender of my truck, like he was just fighting to live and stay awake before collapsing to the ground.

I didn't know what to think. It was crazy. All I wanted to know was if the guy was alive. I could've helped him. Minutes later my mom asked a neighbor if she saw what happened. One of our neighbors said they saw an African-American holding his stomach. He was bleeding out and collapsed to the ground.

Our neighbor didn't call the cops or an ambulance. She said who would miss him. She said if he was a Hispanic, she would've called for help. Me and my mom were furious.

He was a human being. Who cares about the race? I still can't believe racism lives in my neighborhood. The blood is still on the side of my truck. It's been six days since that killing. I think to myself, What if that was me?

The neighborhood hasn't changed. It's been the same. There are still drive-bys, grand thefts, mugging and violence, all kinds. I can't do anything to stop it. I just can't wait to move. Be free, and not having to worry about getting mugged on my way to the corner. I will always remember what I've seen and happened in my neighborhood.

Sometimes you just can't escape reality.

I Am an Immigrant

by Miguel Gianfranco Guzman Valle

I am an immigrant
I am an immigrant from El Salvador
I wonder about being in this foreign country.
I hear people speaking in English, a language unknown to me
I see words on posters that I don't understand
I want to understand when people speak to me
I am an immigrant from El Salvador
I pretend to know when I don't
I feel bad about myself when I am unable to communicate
    and express myself
I touch my throat, trying to pronounce a word in English
I worry that I will never master my adopted language
I cry when I think of not being able to learn it
I am an immigrant from El Salvador
I understand how important it is to learn English
I say that I will speak it someday
I dream of talking and having a fluid conversation
I try to speak and pronounce the words correctly
I hope to be able to speak fluently and effortlessly
I am an immigrant from El Salvador

I Come From

by Michaela Richards

I come from gunshots at 12:00 a.m. that make you hit the floor
I come from a place where every time the doorbell rings I'm afraid to get the door
I come from women who date guys who don't act like grown men
I come from women who let guys with money control them
There aren't fathers where I'm from, just crazy mothers
And friends who can't be friends all because of colors
Twisted fingers and graffiti on the walls
The little girl who sits by the phone waiting for her dad's call
I come from a "Diverse Community" where I'm the only one who's different
I come from a house full of people, but I feel like I'm the only one in it
I come from big thighs and round behinds
Where they show it all off to impress the guys
I come from dark alleys and abandoned buildings
I'm ashamed of where I live, so my friends can't visit
Who cares, though? They're not real anyways
I mean, come on, who really has "friends" these days?
Yeah, we got Homies and Bros and stuff like that
But where I come from they don't really have your back
But wait, you have family. You can depend on them, right?
I thought the same thing, until I finally got sight
Of what they can do to shut down your pride
Make you feel bad and upset all inside.
They don't care if you succeed; they don't want you to do better
They're selfish; they don't want us to succeed together
But overall I believe I come from my sisters
From pinky promises, secrets, and warm hugs and kisses
They're the only reason I keep holding on
To a life that I feel I don't even want.
They are my life and I'll love them forever
Because regardless of where I come from, they continue to make me better

Seeing Who I Am

by Nelvia Marin

I come from a father giving up on his daughter when she was six.
I come from a mother who believes in me.
I come from family always comes first.
I come from a mother who's also my father.
I come from a hard-working mother who accomplishes her dreams.
I come from education is your best weapon in life.
I come from respect has to be built up; you can't have it off the bat.
I come from having a second family, POPS
I come from having someone in prison, my godfather,
To whom my family shows no love, we have left him in the darkness.
I come from having more enemies than friends.
It's okay at the end of the day, they're like a penny, two-faced and worthless.
I come from God gives the hardest battles to the strongest soldiers.
But you will always find your weaknesses.
I come from no pain is forever, but it takes time.
I come from dancing in a room with four mirrors makes my stress suddenly
    go away.
I come from every Saturday it's a turn up day.
I come from writing my feelings on a blank piece of paper to clear my mind.
I come from speak up before it's too late.
I come from stand up for what you believe, don't let ANYONE put you down.
I come from always putting a smile on someone else's face, that's my job.
I come from always trying to keep my life balance.

Written Lines

by J. Murray

I am the sun dappling the water on
A warm morning, December
I am the comfort of my
Corduroy deepening orange
Like a jungle in July
My luscious art
On the boardwalk, food, shops, &
Performances as I pass by
The cool breeze as I skate
At the park until it is
Dark, the feel of the
Sand in my hands
The sound of the waves
While I am on the dock
As the fish wash up
On the beach with my
Board within my reach

When Life Was Perfect

by Chelsea Ramseur

I remember when my life was perfect,

I remember when my life wasn't so perfect.

I remember finding out that my mom had cancer for the first time.

I remember being confused, crying every night, praying to a god that I wasn't even sure existed.

I remember finding out she beat cancer, and thanking that god that I began to believe existed.

I remember hearing my mother crying in her room, calling out to my uncle, saying, "It's bad this time."

I remember finding out that my father was in jail, again.

I remember hugging my mother to console her only to feel a lump on her chest that told me she had cancer again.

I remember not feeling anything anymore except worry about what would become of my life at only thirteen years old.

I was losing my mother, and I had lost my father to the system.

I remember visiting my father in jail, firmly gripping my sister's hand and bracing myself for what I was about to tell him through a glass window.

Mommy died.

I remember moving from county to county, state to state, even having a short stay in another country.

I remember moving to California about four years after Mom died and starting over by myself.

I remember all the lessons I've learned that have shaped me into what I am now.

I Come From

by Alejandra Ruiz

I come from an alcoholic family.

Divided by religion. I come from waking up at 2:00 a.m. to the drunken laughter of my dad and his friends. I come from a grandmother who only calls her son when she wants money. I come from aunts who take advantage of their nieces. I come from a mom who goes to work at 6:00 a.m. and comes home between 8 p.m. and 10 p.m. I come from a dad who loves reptiles and big K-9s. I come from spending my Christmas with neighbors instead of family when my parents were gone. I come from uncles who never visit and when they do they wear smirks slapped on their faces. I come from a family who says we're together. I come from knowing that it's all b.s.

In Her Arms

by Veronica Vargas

The house I lived in for fifteen years is not my home.

My home is not where I live, or where I cook. My home is my mother. Wherever she is, that's home to me.

Many may consider it a cliché, but to me it's completely different. Around two years ago I lost close to all my family I grew up with. It was just another day when my grandma, godfather, and his wife decided to gang up on my mom because my grandma made up a lie, saying that my mom and grandpa were always against her and always bad-mouthing the family. My godfather ended up threatening my mom, and his wife told us to leave the house. We were kicked out of the house we lived in and in just a week had to find a new place to live. When we did, we had no one to rely on, no one to help us out.

At that point in time I thought my whole world was falling apart. That's when I crawled into bed next to my mom and lay my head on her stomach. She said, "What's wrong, my munchichi?"

I shook my head side to side.

Then she put her arm around me and squeezed, "I'm sorry, it's my fault we have no one."

I could hear her breathing getting tighter. I hugged her with one arm and said, "But there's no reason to be sorry. We have each other and that's all I need."

She said, "I love you."

I stayed there for a while longer. I could feel her stomach moving with every breath she took.

At that moment nothing could go wrong. I had everything I ever needed right there, laying my head on her stomach. And that's when it hit me. I've never felt so at home anywhere else—not even in the place I lived for most of my life.

Being with my mom is where I felt safe, where I feel comfortable, like I could breathe again for the first time. It didn't matter if I had no eyeliner on or if my family disowned me. Whenever I was with her I could be myself without being afraid.

When I thought I'd lost it all is when I discovered my home all over again.

War Zone

by Kei-Arri McGruder

I come from where people use their allies as caskets
and children as soldiers
We have our own war in the ghetto
most kids give in to drugs
and other sorts of things
most kids just join a gang
but they'll pack you out
no matter age or gender
this is a war zone
survival of the fittest
and to survive
you must have a pack
or your life can end
just like that

On the Streets of Lennox

by Anthony Rios

I was homeless at the age of eight.

My brothers, sisters, mom, and I lived on the streets because my mom lost her job. We slept in Lennox Park or at Mellows Restaints. It wasn't cool. I could hear police sirens and gunshots every night. I barely slept, and when I did manage to sleep, I had nightmares.

I prayed every night, hoping that we'd be safe until morning. One night I saw my mom doing drugs. That hurt me. And seeing my mom in pain made me cry inside.

I went to school to bring back food for my family. I didn't want to go to class because I was always dirty from sleeping in the park and there was no place for me to shower. I wanted to end my life on the spot, but I didn't because my teacher Ms. Chambers said, "Don't do that, Anthony. You're better than that. If you need anything I'm always here for you."

When my mom said that she was going to take us to our aunt's house in Bakersfield, my brothers, sister, and I were sad because our aunt was mean to us.

My brother Angel received help from a random lady named Judy who saw him on the street and asked, "Where do you live?"

Angel said, "Just take me to Lennox Park."

When Angel arrived at Lennox Park, Judy saw what was going on and said, "You'll stay with me tonight."

My mom told Judy that she could take all us kids home with her that night. "And don't tell the kids they're going to Bakersfield," my mom said.

"Why not?" Judy asked.

"Because they'll run away. They're mistreated there."

"I'll take care of your children for three months," Judy said.

And my mom agreed.

Three months passed. There was no sign of my mom anywhere.

Three months turned into a year. I felt hopeless.

Judy adopted us.

And not long after that my mom came and tried to get us back. But we had to go to court.

The judge awarded custody of all of us to Judy.

I was heartbroken.

I've lived with Judy for the past seven years.

I can't wait to move out of her house and take care of my mom.

And build a future for both of us.

Who We Love

My Parents

by Ia'Leah Cain

When I was younger my mom was not around, but my dad was.

My dad was my favorite person.

But when I was six years old, I had to watch my favorite person die right in front of my face.

The one who told me I was the best thing that ever happened to him.

The one who loved me the most.

The one who took me to get ice cream even when I was bad in class.

So both of my parents were gone.

Well, that's what I thought.

It wasn't until I started getting something called "collect calls" from some lady called "my mom,"

Who I had to look at through a glass window and I couldn't hold or touch her.

I remember when I was 9, and my grandmother would hand me the phone—it was my mom again.

I never understood why she had to get off the phone so fast.

When I turned 14, my mom came home. It felt as if I hadn't seen her forever.

It had gotten to the point where I called my grandmother Mom.

Then my mother disappeared again. By then I understood she was back in prison, and it hurt me because I heard horrible stories about prison.

But when she came back home, it felt good, natural, as it had been so long ago.

Dear God

by Melissa Nava

Dear God,

Virginia R. Flores is my mother. She seems to bear the weight of the world on her shoulders, but to carry it more lightly than I think I would.

I see her balancing dialysis, home, money, no money, and friends who no longer make time to see her, and I send up this prayer for her. She is lonely, loving God. She would like company but doesn't want her friends to feel sorry for her and also doesn't want to make time for new relationships because her waking hours are already full. She's a single mother. She walks when gas is too expensive for the car and doesn't buy herself new clothes just so her kids can have food on the table and a roof over their shoulders. This is not how her life started out, but circumstances changed from her life of privilege to this life she embraces so fully. Her life is difficult and she seems so tired most of the time, but I'm inspired by the love she has for her children. Give her strength to put in long hours each day, the ability to maintain her long loving life at home, and the deepest knowledge in her heart that you love her. Please help her remember that you are there for her when she is feeling sad and help her remember that she has a longer life to live and that you don't need her up there yet. Please God, that's all I wish for. Amen.

Portrait of Melissa Nava, © Hannah Schatzle

All My Life

by Angel De La Cruz

All my life I've been raised by my mom who played the role of mother and father.

Since I was five years old, my father has been in and out of prison. I last saw him almost ten years ago, when I was eight.

My dad was pretty chill and sometimes a nice guy, at least to me. But he went to prison for domestic violence and robbery. All of his bad behavior was caused by his alcohol addiction.

When I was a boy, sometimes I was afraid just to speak to him, and I would stand in the corner shaking because of his temper.

My dad is 5'7" tall, with medium brown skin, black hair, and black eyes. His eyes look just like mine.

He was gang-related, but he's no longer involved with gang activity. He quit that when he learned the hard way—behind bars.

I didn't write to my dad while he was in prison, and for a while I convinced myself I didn't care about him.

Even without a dad around, I played it straight. In high school I played on the football team for three years, and I earned good grades and participated in clubs. The entire time my mom was by my side. She took 100% of the responsibility for raising me right.

I always wanted a real dad who would toughen me up, play catch with me on the football field or at the park. I always wanted a real dad who would play video games with me or give me those guy lectures and life advice. You know, little stuff I never had.

People used to assume I'd turn out like him. "Oh Angel, he's going to be just like his dad. He's got his genes."

But those people were shocked. I became a bright, educated young man. Again, because my mom was there for me.

And because she was there watching over me, I always hung out with positive people. I never wanted to be the guy who was mean. I wanted to be a decent person who got along well with everyone.

After all I've seen my father go through, I've taught myself to be disciplined, respectful, patient, and kind.

My friends often ask me how I forged my own path, one so unlike my father's. And I always say, "Stay humble, hungry, and dedicated to something or someone you love, because with these virtues, good things will come." All that I have seen and all that I have done make me realize I'm a good guy.

Portrait of Angel De La Cruz © Hannah Schatzle

His Blood Runs Through Me

by Kat Secaida

Today in a courthouse somewhere in Los Angeles, my father is facing a judge, and I am in my English class worrying about him.

I wonder why I have to have such a screwed-up father. I mean, I hear my friends talk about their dads who take them places; who are there for their birthdays. Most nights I cry myself to sleep fearing one day my father will die from his addiction. He's an alcoholic.

I know my dad loves me, and I love him deeply, but I can't deal with this anymore.

I wake every morning or in the middle of the night thinking, "What's the next call my mother's going to receive? How's she going to break the news to my sister and me this time?"

I've heard my dad talk about how much pain he's in and I tell him to go to the doctor and he says, "No!"

He acts like everything is fine. He acts like he never ruins anything.

Every time he calls, I think, "What if he's drunk? Should I pick up?" Half the time I don't. And I wonder if that hurts him. But then I think, "F__ it, it hurts me too!"

He has one life and he's destroying it. He has a family who cares about him, but he keeps chasing his addiction.

I wake every morning or in the middle of the night thinking, "How does he live his life like this? What goes through his mind?"

I know one day he will die and I won't be ready for that. Just as I wasn't ready to hear that he was sent to jail for the second time.

Sometimes I wish I didn't have a father.

I know if he goes to jail, he'll get help. But I know how it is inside. Like my father, I've been arrested.

But today as he faces the judge, I feel he's not my problem. But at the same time, I know he is.

Because he's my father.

His blood runs through me.

I Have Always Been Searching for a Father

by Anthony Rios

I have always been alone searching for a father, but it never happened.

Every night and day I have been praying to see him.

I have been crying for so long.

I was lost in the world, doing drugs, joining a gang, just looking for a father figure.

He fades away.

I learned things the hard way, by seeing my mom working so hard to give my brothers, sisters, and me a bite to eat every day.

Every night I listen to my mom cry.

I felt bad because I thought it was my fault he left.

When I saw him in jail, he said, "Sorry."

But I didn't listen to him. I was so mad I couldn't forgive him because he wasn't there when I needed him.

But I learned to keep my head up and how to forgive my father.

I thank God for changing my life. Without God in my life, I would be lost.

The King

by Joslyn Stevenson

You screwed up,
Man, look at you
Locked up again
Four more years in the pen
Man, I gotta say,
I had a feeling it'd happen this way
Too high to realize the guy you were slanging to
Was more undercover than you
He caught you slippin' and now you're gone
What's sad is that when you do get out,
You gonna head to that same crack house
Put that same pipe to your mouth
And whip that same lighter out
I guess you don't learn nothing
In the pen
Just how to shoot dice
Protect your life
And maybe think about
Not going back in
So you can live a free life
And continue to sin

Trouble

by Joslyn Stevenson

In and out of prison,
But never not high.
Been making bad decisions
Since your dad left, and your
Mom died.
Criss-crossing on your train
tracks of thoughts
Wondering if standing in the middle
was for you or not.

Innocent

by Mariana Hernandez

There's this story I can never forget.

In fifth grade, I received a note to report to the principal's office. I couldn't imagine what I had done wrong.

As soon as I entered the office, my eyes met those two policemen sitting with their legs crossed. They never took their eyes off me. I felt intimidated, attacked.

These two approached me and asked me some questions.

"What does your dad do when you guys argue?"

"Does he lock you up in the bathroom by yourself?"

"Does he get you in trouble a lot, sweetie?"

"What does he say to your sisters when they argue?"

"He never laid hands on you, did he?"

I tried to answer these questions as fast as I could so I could get it over with. The only words that came out of my mouth were: "We never even fight."

When I came home later that day, I learned why the police had showed up at my school. My aunt reported my father for child abuse. This didn't surprise me. My mom's side of the family never got along with my dad's side, and my aunt wanted my dad out of the picture.

When my aunt reported my dad I was too young to know what was happening. But I felt lost, confused, scared, angry.

Two days later, a social worker visited my house and asked me more questions about my dad. The social worker was a female in her 30s. She stayed for two hours questioning me and my two older sisters. My sisters entered their room first, along with the lady. Then it was my turn ... I was nervous. I had to enter the room alone and I sat on my sister's bed as the woman sat next to me with a clipboard in her hand. I avoided eye contact, looking down at my fingers.

"Has Daddy ever laid his hands on you?"

"Who gives you baths?"

Those are the only questions I remember.

My dad never hurt or touched me, nor did he hurt or touch my two older sisters.

Because of my aunt's allegations, the social worker didn't trust me to be alone with my dad. For about a week, whenever my mom was at work, my aunt from my dad's side had to watch me.

To this day I'm still upset by the experience and I know my own father was always innocent.

In time, the social worker realized my dad had done nothing wrong and she left and never returned.

Today, my mom still keeps in touch with my aunt and believes me and my sisters should give her another chance.

I will always care for her because she's family. But I've lost respect for her.

Engraved in My Memory

by Grecia Jara

I checked the time, 1:00 a.m. As my eyes glanced around the room, all I could see was my family, with expressions I can't even describe. There was a sort of sadness in the entire room. I scrambled across the room and sat in my chair, pulled my knees up, and wrapped my arms around them. Something was wrong, more wrong than I realized. I could feel it. My mom muttered something I didn't quite understand as she went back to my dad's side. "What's wrong?" I asked. She hurried to my side. "Please go get some more ice from the waiting room, honey."

"All right." As I got up I felt something was completely wrong, but went to do what my mom had asked me to do anyway. I struggled to get a grip on myself as I walked down the busy hallway. Once I reached the ice machine, I felt a sharp pain in my stomach, a gut feeling that something bad was about to happen. I almost dropped everything I had in my hands and started running down the hallway back to my dad's hospital room. Once I got to the door I hesitated, scared of what I would see, what I would hear, of what to think. As I finally worked up the courage to walk inside the room, the first face I saw was my mother's. There was something buried in her eyes that I couldn't be sure of—and it scared me. I stared for another minute, shocked, paralyzed. I could feel something, panic maybe, building up in my chest. My whole body went numb. I couldn't feel anything below my neck. My knees must have started to shake because the walls of the room were suddenly wobbling. I could hear my heart pounding faster than normal behind my ears. I closed my eyes and tried to breathe normally, tried to pretend it wasn't happening, that it was all just a dream and none of it had ever happened. "Just a dream," I told myself. I forced myself to open my eyes, nothing seemed to go away. I hoped that I was fainting, but to my disappointment, I didn't lose consciousness.

I walked up to the side of my dad's bed and held his hand, one last time. His hands were warm, and I knew if I wanted to say something to him I had to say it to him now. "I love you," I whispered.

I felt his hand squeeze my hand. Even though he was sleeping, he could still hear us. But his grip slowly started to fade. I looked up at him. I saw him take his last breath, and just like that, he was gone. It felt as if the waves of pain that had only lapped at me before were now reared high up and had washed over my head, and I felt as if I was never going to be able to resurface. He was there for my very first breath, and I was there for his last.

I have learned to not take every day I get for granted, but as a gift. To cherish every single moment I have with my family and the ones that I love no matter the circumstances, especially my mother who had to switch gears to become a mother and father combined just to care for me.

Say You're Sorry

by Anonymous

I was about thirteen years old when the truth finally came out. I was outside when my mom called me into the kitchen.

She was crying. And I didn't know why.

She asked me a couple of questions, some questions I never thought she would ask. But finally she said, "Has anyone ever touched you?"

"No," I said.

"Please tell me the truth, it's okay," she replied. She began to name men and asked if they had ever touched me or if I knew if they ever touched any of my cousins. I heard her say her brothers' names, then she started naming her cousins. Then she said HIS name. I froze.

And I came out with the truth. I wasn't sure what to say, maybe I should have lied, but I didn't. I was living in fear of him for years and now was my chance to tell everyone what was going on.

"Yes, he did, it was him, it's true, he touched her," I admitted.

But she didn't believe me, or she didn't want to. "This is serious, are you sure of what you're telling me?" she asked with a look with disbelief. "Why didn't you tell me before?"

And I began to cry. Why would I lie about something this serious? Didn't she know how afraid I was to say anything about it? We told my grandma about it, but we were just little girls, who would believe us?

I told her how it happened—how my cousins and I were playing in the garage when he walked in. How most of us were able to get out, but she stayed in there. Then my mom said, "Okay, don't tell anyone about this."

That's the day my family fell apart. Never again did I see my two aunts in the same room again. My mom's sister, the mother of the cousin who was the victim and my uncle's sister never talked again.

Never again did my family give one another a sincere hug. For a while we didn't see that part of my family—my uncle and his sisters.

He was in jail for three years. His sisters were always trying to get him out. And they hated my cousin's mom for putting him in there. My cousin's mom was isolated from her own brothers and sisters because not everyone agreed with what she did.

He hurt us so he deserved to be in jail, but then, growing up, all we were taught was "forgive and forget." It wasn't for revenge that I wanted him in there, but he needed to learn his lesson. He needed to know that what he did was wrong and that he shouldn't have tried to deny it. It was his word against my cousin's word.

My mom finally came around and realized he had to pay for what he did. She no longer tried to defend him.

If it was another man who had done what he did, no one would want him out of jail.

But he did what he did; he hurt my cousin. She is now an outcast from half my family. My mom's siblings fell apart because of him. Eventually they talked things out and apologized for making things harder on her. Unfortunately, he never apologized.

To this day when we run into my uncle and his sisters, we hug and talk, but in the end, I feel the hate there.

A Mistake

by Nelvia Marin

3 men
1 down
A coward
And a man with bloody hands
A gun set off a bullet to the chest
The warmness and pain this man must feel on his chest
The pain of the family, you no longer have a son
Just pain
The pain of a wife with no love, a child with no father
Just because a coward was on the scene
A man is stuck in the darkness
Needs love to brighten up his days
But will never find love again
A mistake took it all
A man stands alone
So many "friends" who do not have his back
Family support none
So many stories about your mistake
That gets me confused
I need things to get cleared up
So I can understand
This unclear story about you
It's just pain in the prison system.

Portrait of Nelvia Marin © Hannah Schatzle

She's Not Gone

by Nichole Landaverde

I've never given thought of how life without a mother would be. Kids are supposed to outlive their parents. But why at age thirteen did I feel the need to "grow up." I have a father, I have a brother. I just had this distinctive bond with my mother. I mean, she gave birth to me. I am half of her. No, I'm not exaggerating. I just never feel whole. Always hoping she is the next person to walk through the door. I know people go through worse, but it's appropriate to be narrow-minded at times.

It was all so sudden, one moment she was peacefully watching TV, next moment red lights were flashing outside our home. I avoided focusing on her lying on the paramedics' bed as they took her. Deep down I knew something was out of the ordinary. She had gone to the hospital by ambulance before, but I never felt this feeling. I was the one who had to contact my father, to describe the last half-an-hour. I felt achy and gnawy, trying not to concentrate on what could possibly be going on in the hospital.

Waiting at my home for what seemed like days was unendurable. I tried contacting my father but caught the answering machine each time. I knew something was off-target as soon as he messaged me back. He never texts me. It was stinging as he walked in with swollen red eyes. I knew he was tender, but I found myself not caring. I hugged him anyway, feeling as if I were the parent comforting a child. No words can describe his appearance. All I could think was, "What the f***?" She had an artery clog, also called a heart attack. She had trouble breathing normally as she lay on the bed. My aunt accompanied her to the hospital. It is hard to this day to even communicate with my aunt about the last minutes she spent with her sister. Why ask, do I really want to know?

It's not that I didn't believe the news of my mother passing away, but why? I did understand the concept of death, even of her life ending. Everyone dies at some point. That's the thing about death; it has its own time.

I don't dream of her. I don't talk about her. I write to her, stacks of unread letters to her. It's difficult to think of a future without a mother's unconditional love.

Do I cry? Move on? Either way, nothing's going to bring her back. I see the effect she left on my father. His light is gone. He moves so weakly. Before she died, he woke up joyfully singing the same song every morning. He is a happy-feel person. But now he always has a worried look. I can't say I don't feel empathy, but I certainly feel his sympathy towards me. That's not what I want. I don't talk to him unless it's about sports or cars. I've lived with my father and brother for more than two years now, and every day I crave girl talk. I see characteristics in me that weren't there before. Is it terrible to feel a little relieved? She knew secrets that I was ashamed of. Knowing she would never speak of, but I worried she thought differently of me. That doesn't make it right.

My brother is shut down about his feelings—laughing all the time, like always. Knowing there is bitterness deep down in both of us. *I know I'm not the only one who felt.* I'm reminded every damn day of her due to my personality, which I'm grateful to have received. She has affected everyone she knew so much, we all speak more wisely with her words. She's not gone.

Defining Myself

by Angelee Velasquez

I was raised by one woman.

A strong woman.

Who told me that a man's approval does not need to define me.

I come from a woman, a strong woman, who played the role of both parents in my life.

My father left me, the first time, when I was six.

He said he didn't want anything to do with me.

What can a six-year-old do to make a parent shirk his responsibility?

Like every girl, I deserved the love of a father. One can't find that connection anywhere else.

My mom is the reason I am who I am today. A strong, independent young woman who will be successful. I will overcome my father's absence and the naysayers who surround me.

My paternal grandmother once said, "You're just like your mom. You'll never get anywhere. You'll end up pregnant just like your mother."

She also prophesized that I would not graduate from high school.

I believe that everyone has a purpose.

I believe my purpose is to inspire and encourage little girls, teenage girls, and young women. To show them that just because one's past was difficult, it doesn't mean that the rest of life has to be just has hard.

I am here to show young women that it is possible to be successful without degrading one's body. I know that is my mission.

My mother taught me that knowledge is power, and I believe that.

I also know that being a parent is difficult.

And I thank my mother for always guiding me in the right direction.

For wanting the best for me.

Even for spoiling me.

I am from a strong, beautiful woman.

And I intend to be just like her.

Portrait Angelee Velasquez © Hannah Schatzle

My Uncle's DUI

by Alejandra Ruiz

A few weeks ago my Uncle Esquiel was in a car crash. He sped through a red light somewhere in Hollywood. The driver from the car he crashed into was hurt, but not seriously. My uncle was arrested for driving under the influence and spent two nights in jail.

His small green four-door Toyota was totally trashed. The front of the car was smashed in so badly that even if the exterior damage could be repaired, the car would still be useless due to all the twisted metal under the hood.

If it were up to me, I would have let my uncle stay in jail until his court date. I would not have bailed him out, because my Uncle Esquiel, like my dad, is an alcoholic. And like my dad, he promises to quit drinking but never does.

Shortly after my uncle's DUI arrest, my mom warned my dad that if he ever is arrested for a DUI, that night, right then and there, she will sign papers to have him sent back to Mexico.

I worry all the time about my dad drinking and driving—even if he's had only one sip of booze.

I want him to quit.

And every night I hope that he's learned his lesson before something tragic actually happens.

When Will He Get Out?

by Kat Secaida

The day my whole life changed was when my father was jailed for the second time.

For some reason, his first arrest didn't hit me as hard as the second one.

My father was sent to jail on January 4, 2015. I didn't find out about that until January 8.

Not a great way to start the new year, with my dad imprisoned. On the other hand, he was never around anyway.

On the morning of January 8, my mother, crying, came into my room. I asked her what was wrong and she said, "Nothing. I'm okay."

I looked at her.

"Well," I said, "don't come into my room crying and then you won't tell me what's wrong."

She caught her breath and said something like, "You know when you break the law you have to go to jail because ..."

I cut her off.

"So my dad's in jail again?"

I wanted to cry, but then I thought, "This isn't something new."

I kept myself from crying, but I couldn't keep myself from feeling sad and disappointed.

I asked my mom how long he'd been locked up. She said, "Four days."

I exploded.

"You lied to me. You said he had changed."

Then I caught myself and quieted down.

I've learned something from my father's arrests. I learned that holding a grudge doesn't hurt the person I'm angry at, it only hurts me. I'm the one who has to wake up every morning and try to stay positive.

"No more fears," I told myself. "No more holding on to grudges. Stay focused. Stay positive. Look on the bright side."

Even when I hurt.

Especially when I hurt.

My Mothers' Daughter

by Veronica Vargas

I am a daughter. That is what makes up most of my identity.

Not only am I a daughter to my mother but to my Grandma Rosa as well.

I remember when I was younger, my mom, brother, father, and I lived in a two-bedroom house with my grandparents, Rosa and Jose. My grandma was always in and out of hospitals.

One day we were sitting on the couch in the living room where she always seemed to be. The couch was brown and tan and faced the window looking out on the front lawn. She sat there crying. I lay my head on her shoulder and wiped away her tears.

"What's wrong, Grandma?" I asked.

"*Nada, mija,*" she faked a smile to match her answer.

"I know something's wrong, tell me!"

"You're the only one who loves me, I don't know what will happen when you're no longer here with me. Who will still care for me? I can't go on without my little girl," she said.

"I'll always be there …" my voice cracked. "Maybe not always physically, but in heart. We'll never leave one another alone, okay?"

It was in that moment that I knew I was more than just a granddaughter to her, but her daughter as well. I wanted to keep her happy.

Not long after that I lost my grandma after her open-heart surgery failed. I didn't have the chance to say good-bye, and I still feel that my right to do so was unfairly taken away.

But I'm lucky enough to still have my momma, Norma, here with me, and I'm scared I could lose her any day since she's heading down the same path as her mom.

Last month my momma had a high blood pressure attack. My brother was sleeping on the couch, and I was sitting alone eating dinner when I heard my mom call for me.

"Vero, help me," she tried to yell.

I ran. She lay on the floor, shivering. All I could think was that I couldn't lose my only mom. Who would I live to impress? Who would I look after and have look after me?

My brother ran and helped her up. Her toes were purple, her breath unsteady. She asked my brother and me to lie there with her while she cried.

"I couldn't leave my babies without saying bye," she said.

"*Vero, my munchichi,* when I go, you need to be there for your brother and dad. Keep an eye on them and make sure they behave. I'm sorry." She hugged me tightly as she spoke.

I couldn't respond because the thought of losing my mom made me ill. I wanted my grandma to still be alive, and I wanted my mom to be well.

My life revolves around the love my mom offers me, the support she always willingly gives. I am who I am because I am the daughter to the two strongest women I know, Norma Uribe and Maria Rosa Placencia. Although one is no longer here and the other is just taking things day by day, I remain a daughter to both, day and night.

A daughter represents her mother. And in this case I represent two. They taught me to be open-minded, strong, kindhearted, and independent. I am who they raised me to be.

I've always known I was super close to both my mom and grandma, but it wasn't until I lost my grandma and almost lost my mom that I realized I'd be completely lost without being a daughter to them.

And what I need to know is that they both will always love me and that I won't be left alone.

Unexpected Trip to Happiness

by Brittany

It's 6:30 a.m. on a Wednesday morning. I should be going to school but my mom says I need to go with her—on a road trip. I ask why and she says, "You'll find out." We get dressed, pack snacks for the road and pillows in case I get sleepy. We get on the road and I ask my mom to stop at McDonald's so I can use the restroom. She grows irritated because I didn't go before we left the house. I use the restroom and buy a McChicken, then climb back into the car. Again I ask my mom where we are going and still she will not tell me. We enter the freeway and drive.

Three hours pass, and I peek out the window and see nothing but dirt, a few trees, cacti, and tumbleweeds. I still don't know where we are or where we are headed. All I know is that I am far from home and I don't like it. We finally spot some civilization; a restaurant or two, a liquor store, and a little shop selling antiques. We pull into the restaurant, grab a bite to eat, and then get back on the road. It is about 10:30 a.m. when we pull into a huge parking lot facing a few giant cement buildings gated off with barbed-wire-topped fences. I ask why we are here and she refuses to answer.

She says, "And now we wait." We wait. An hour passes—nothing. I ask, "Where are we?"

"Baby," she says, "we are somewhere that I never ever want to be again." I can tell she is on the verge of breaking down but staying strong for my sake.

Another hour passes. Still nothing. I grow impatient; I am tired of waiting for something I don't even know what I am waiting for. I want to go home. A white van pulls up and out of curiosity I stare. These are the first humans I've seen in five or six hours. A bald Caucasian male, 5'11" maybe 6 feet tall, gets out of the driver's seat. He wears a tan uniform, black boots, black hip band with a .45 on his right hip, a bunch of keys on the left, and a couple pairs of handcuffs in back. He opens the side door and lets four men out—two Latinos, one African-American, and one Caucasian. But there is another man facing backwards who is still in the van. My mom says, "Baby, get out of the car when the others walk away." I say, "Okay," then wait a couple of minutes as I watch the others reunite with their families.

I climb out of the car as the sheriff closes the door and walk to the rear of the van. He opens the back door and lets a man out; he uncuffs him and says, "Have a nice day." The man chuckles and says, "Gee, thanks."

The man who comes out of the van is not who I expected. Although I recognize his voice he doesn't look at all like he did when I last saw him. He is weak, pale, and thin, as if he hasn't eaten in days. I look at him from the ground up, overwhelmed with emotions. I run to him and with tears coming down jump in his arms. No words, just tears and happiness. I finally have my dad back in my arms, and he is holding me in his.

I Grew Up in a Happy Home

by Michelle Montano

I grew up in what seemed to be a happy home.

I was always smiling, rarely cried, and no one ever seemed to argue. Since I was a child, my mom, dad, and big brother, Jeremiah, have been the center of my world. My mom and dad were deeply in love, even after twenty years of marriage.

Even though we didn't live in the best neighborhood, they always found a way to make me laugh and see the best in every situation. It wasn't until I turned twelve that it all fell apart.

On May 9, 2010, my daddy was sent to prison and was given two life sentences. My mom broke down as soon as he was gone. She fell deep into depression and she wouldn't speak to either me or my brother. She was lost in her sorrow. I felt desperate for my daddy's hugs and I actually missed listening to his lectures and him telling me how proud he knew I would one day make him.

Jeremiah became more than just my brother, he was now my best friend and the only reason I had left to keep trying. He and I did everything together. He wasn't the best role model, but he looked out for me and despite being eight years older than me, he always treated me as his equal, never judged my decisions.

By thirteen I was watching him do drugs, gangbang, and gamble. I moved into his two-bedroom apartment with him and his girlfriend. At first, I felt at peace and safe. Jeremiah taught me everything I needed to survive.

One day we were sitting on the porch with his friends. I remember Jeremiah giving me a long speech that ended with, "Michelle, one day I want to see you make it out of the 'hood, even if I don't make it out with you."

All I could think was, "Why wouldn't you make it out with me?"

He made me promise I'd be successful. When his friends left, I shared my thoughts and questions with him. He told me that people like him don't make it anywhere. I couldn't quite understand, but I didn't question him anymore.

At fifteen, I was seemingly doing well in school, even though I had been kicked out of three high schools in two years. My brother seemed happy, living life day by day as usual.

July 17, 2013, around 4:30 p.m., I was walking home from school as I did every day. As I neared home, I could see an ambulance and police cars. I saw my family and neighbors crying. When I asked what was going on, the police pulled me to the side and asked for my I.D. They interrogated me for five minutes before they realized I was Jeremiah's sister.

Then they told me that my brother had been shot. Killed.

My body became stiff, weak. He was gone, shot dead by an enemy on his own porch. At age 23. The very porch where we shared laughs and enjoyed each other's company. I didn't cry. Not a tear dripped out of me because he taught me never to let people know when I am hurt.

I walked closer to the yellow tape and I could see his feet sticking out of the white cover they'd put over him. The puddle of blood surrounding his body seemed deeper than the ocean. I ran and tried to hug him one last time, but the police pulled me away. The next day I moved in with my mom. She was still depressed and quiet, now more than before. I noticed my mom's eyes had changed. The once strong and joyful superwoman had turned into a disconnected, fragile human being. My uncle moved in with us to help my mom out. Mommy was no longer here, Daddy was taken away, and my brother was gone.

Every Monday at 4:00 p.m. I visit my brother's grave and sit and talk as if he were sitting right beside me. I laugh at the things I imagine he would say to me and cry because I can't hear him saying them.

I pretend we are on the porch, and that makes me feel like I'm home.

I Am His Granddaughter

by Leslie Mateos

I define myself as a granddaughter. A granddaughter who wants to be just like her grandfather.

I met my grandfather when I was six. The first time I saw him I told my mother, "I want to be like him. I want to be like your dad, like Marcos Martinez."

I spent my two months in Mexico following him around. I would step in his footprints in the dirt when we walked to the store. One day my grandfather took me to his ranch and sat me down on a rock. He stood in front of me and said, "So your mother told me you want to be like me. Is that true?"

"Yes, I do," I said, proud of admitting it.

"Well *mi niña*, if you want to be like me you'll have to be a hard worker and accomplish many things in life."

"Can you tell me the things you've accomplished? I want to do the same things."

Two months passed by quickly. Soon it was time to go back to Los Angeles. It didn't take long before my father was deported and we moved to Mexico. We spent two years in Mexico, but I was happy because my grandfather was always around. I visited him every day after school. I'd tell him everything I learned.

My parents started having problems, so my mother decided we would move back to L.A. I cried for a week knowing that I'd be leaving behind the two people I loved most, my father and grandfather. My mother told me not to worry because even though we would be far away, there would always be communication and that I'd be able to go back and visit.

My mom didn't lie about having communication. I called my grandpa every two weeks. They were short calls, but it didn't matter as long as I was able to hear my grandpa's voice. As I grew older I would ask my mom when I would be able to visit my grandparents. She never gave an exact answer.

In the summer of 2010 my dream came true. I returned to Mexico and stayed with my grandparents. I spent the time with my grandpa. We watched TV, took short walks, and I ate breakfast, lunch, and dinner every day sitting next to him. Again time flew and soon it was time for me to return to L.A. On my last night there my grandpa called me to sit next to him while he was lying in bed.

"Leslie, do you remember when you said you wanted to be like me?"

"Yes, and I haven't changed my mind. I want to be a hard worker like you."

"Well, I've got one last thing to tell you. I want you to pay attention, because it's something that I learned as I grew up."

"I'm listening."

"*La feria se gasta, la fama se termina, mas lo que haces en la vida a ninguno se le olvida. Cuida tus semillas hasta el día de tu partida. Si quieres ser como yo demuéstrame que puedes.*"

"*Money is spent, fame ends, but what you do in life no one forgets. Take care of your seeds up to the day of your death. If you want to be like me prove to me that you can be.*"

His words expressed something deep, but I was confused, wondering what seeds had to do with me and why he was telling me this.

I simply replied, "Yes Grandpa, don't worry, I will."

Two months later my grandfather passed away. I cried day and night. One night after crying I rose from bed and went to the living room. I stood in front of the altar and in front of my grandfather's portrait.

"*Abuelito,* I promised I'd be like you, and here in front of the altar I swear to you that I'll be like you. Everything you wished for I will obtain. I will take care of my seeds (kids) the same way you did. I'll always remember you."

I feel like I am his only granddaughter because I was the one closest to him. I am my grandfather's daughter, and I will make him proud. I will obtain what he always wished, making his house big and keeping his ranch full of crops.

Why Don't You Let Me Help You?

by Nichole Landaverde

Don't you understand my arms are wide open and my ears are just
 for listening?
You've told me hints of the unspoken but crave knowledge that's
 more than skin deep.
I won't accept the fact you are breaking and I am standing here
 pretending to be blind to it.
I won't feel sympathy, because I know that's not what you want.
I just need you to need me.
Trust me.
Not for my benefit or selfish reasons
Because I believe you need to be listened to.
Why am I in your shadows when it comes to expressing emotions?
Look at me, for heaven's sake.
I am here for you.
Talk to me; pour your heart out to me.
I won't accept the fact that you are perfectly fine.
Your eyes speak for what your mouth's not saying.
I care, damn it.
Why don't you let me help you?

Ordinary Night

by Anthony Cortez

I sat at my kitchen table late one Sunday night. I was typing my final chapter for an essay for U.S. History. The house was silent just as I like it when I'm writing. My thoughts and ideas were flowing freely onto paper without much difficulty.

The house phone rang loud enough for all to hear. I didn't move a muscle, for I thought my sister or grandmother would answer the phone since they were nearer. I suddenly felt a horrid feeling. I stood and walked to the phone, not wanting to make much noise. When I picked up the receiver's cold exterior it sent a strange sensation down my spine.

"Hello," I said in a curious voice.

"Anthony, it's grandmamma." She spoke in a slow, soft voice.

She had never called at such a late hour just to talk, and I wondered what was wrong.

"You may want to sit. What I'm about to say is probably going to hurt."

"What's wrong?" I asked.

"Your Uncle Danny passed away this morning," she said in a shaky, raspy voice.

I dropped the phone, placed my head in my hands. I tasted the saltiness of my tears.

"Anthony, Anthony, are you there?" she asked.

I slowly picked up the phone, barely able to place it against my ear. "I'll call you tomorrow," I said and hung up before I could hear her response.

I sat with my head in my hands for maybe an hour or two. I don't remember. I cried and cried. I could not believe my uncle was gone. I would never lay eyes on him again. When I forced myself to stand, I walked to my room in darkness, unable to see the path that lay before me. Once in my room I plopped onto my bed.

When my eyes closed, all I could see was Danny's handsome face. His caramel skin tone, soft, light brown eyes, and shaggy black hair. His smile and eyes taking me back to all the fond memories we shared. They raced through my mind like a movie.

I remember when I was five years old. He would take me to a small liquor store with whitewashed walls and old rusted bars on all the windows. I was able to get anything I wanted. I felt special and engulfed in pleasure every time he chose me out of all my cousins who begged him to take them to the store.

Whenever I was feeling sad, he would buy me a box of Pop Pop Poppers, small bundles of rocks that contain silver fulminate. They made a loud popping noise when thrown against the ground. We would throw handfuls of them, laughing together.

He taught me to live in the moment. What matters most is what is happening in this moment. I shouldn't worry about yesterday, because that was past. Tomorrow is a mystery, and you can always improve yesterday. I live my life as if today is my last. I put one hundred percent into any task I embark upon. I exceed every possibility before I ask for help because I hate to give up. When I do, I feel as if I am giving up on myself.

Not a Day Goes by
That I Don't Think of You

by Marianne Valencia

Not a day goes by that I don't think of you
When you left, I was ten
You took me with you
I fell into deep depression

Every day I thought about you. Your laugh, voice, and your bear hugs
I remember going to work with you and to the beach on summer days. I
    remember your smell, your smile.

I remember how red your eyes were after a long day at work in construction. I
    remember that you could not do anything without drinking, on a daily basis.

I thought, "Why did you walk out completely, without a goodbye note, a letter, a
    call?"

Were you ashamed that you couldn't provide for my mom, sister, brother, and me?

How could you leave three kids behind? Daisy, the oldest, Andrew, the middle
    child, and me, your baby.

How do you live with yourself?

Do you miss me like I have missed you?

I went through hell growing up always changing schools as we moved. It was hard
    to make new friends.

Most importantly always leaving you.
I used to tell you how my day went and how I was feeling.
You were my best friend.

My mom says I shouldn't be sad over you.
She says you don't deserve my tears.
I tried calling you every day to figure out what went wrong, but you never
    answered.

In 2013 I went to San Francisco to see you after Thanksgiving. I was 16 years old.
    You acted so cold towards me.

How could you front with a Grinch smile, ear to ear, and your children bawling
    their eyes out with tears?

I did this so that you know I've never stopped crying.

Portrait of Marianne Valencia © Hannah Schatzle

I Remember

by Bianca Lopez

I remember when the cops would come to my house looking for my brother,
almost breaking down the walls.

I remember when my parents wouldn't tell me what was going on because they
said I was too young to understand.

I remember late nights when I would hear the police sirens roaming the streets,
me wondering if something had happened to my brother.

I remember when they took my brother to prison for something he didn't even
do.

I remember the phone calls saying he misses and loves us.

I remember the long waiting lines just to get on a bus to visit my brother at L.A.
county jail.

I remember the days he wasn't here as a brother like he should be.

I remember having nothing to say but that I have a brother in jail.

Sincerely, a Daughter

by Veronica Vargas

Dear God, you have blessed me with an angel.
You have opened my eyes to what eternal love is.
But now, she's sick, and I'm afraid that soon you will take her away.
My mother is my sun; my world revolves around her.
So I thank you every day and night when I look to my side and still see her there.
Depression and pain engulf her.
So now I kneel before you and beg once again to numb this because it's driving
  her insane.
Turn sobbing into laughter.
Turn sorrow to joy.
She is your child; I am her fruit.
I pray and I ask that you'll lift her spirits, to help her through her darkest days.
Never alone, forever loved
Protect my angel.
Take her beneath your arms.

Grateful

by Irvin Gutierrez-Lopez

Father God who is up in the heavens, I come to You today to ask for forgiveness. I've made choices and said many things that I wish I'd never done. If only there was a way to undo those decisions I've made, but I thank You God for keeping me here. There are many people out in the world who made decisions like me and lost their way. I thank You for keeping me alive all this time when there were times in life I could've been dead or lost. The path You have lead me towards is a great path. I pursue my dream of becoming a screenwriter and directing with You by my side, I know everything is possible for you. I thank You for the people you've put around me who give me great support and smiles and great advice when I'm feeling down. I also thank You for taking away the friends that brought me no good and others who've hurt me. I sometimes still find it hard to understand why they left, but only You know why they're gone. I'm happy for the life You have given me and the family You have a provided me with. I can always count on them whenever I need them. Father God I am grateful for everything in my life and I ask that you keep me going towards the right path, and if I fall I ask that You pick me back up. In Your heavenly name I pray, Amen.

Lend Them Some Angels

by Michaela Richards

Dear Lord,
I come to you to ask today
Because I do not know another way
That if you have spare angels above
To send one to each of the ones I love.

For my mom, dear Lord, she needs a fighter, an angel that can walk through fire
The angel with the sharpest spear. An angel who has no fears
Because my mom faces new devils every day.
I think she needs an angel to tell her it's okay.
An angel with a soft side too
For the days she starts to feel blue
An angel that understands that some days are not so bright
An angel that can walk with her through darkness and through light.
An angel that's tough, but still is full of love
Tell me, God, do you have any angels like these above?

Another angel I need, you know,
Is an angel to help my sister grow
A guardian angel to help her decide
If the things that she does are actually right
An angel to steer her clear of the wrongs.
An angel to keep my little sister strong.
Because the truth is, Lord, she's growing up
And to live in this world she has to be tough.
She needs an angel to help her stand her ground,
Especially for the times when I'm not around
An angel to walk beside her, dear Lord,
My sister needs an angel to guide her.

And, Lord, don't forget to send an angel for my best friend,
An angel that stands tall and never bends.
Lately her heart is full of anger
Lord, she needs an angel that will change her

Back to the friend that I've always known,
I need her to know that she's not alone.
Her angel needs to be a reflection of who she used to be
Because I need the angel to bring my best friend back to me.

Now Chelsea, she needs an angel to protect her heart
Because she's down for everyone, but looking out for herself is the hard part.
She needs an angel to match her heart of gold
Because she truly is the best person I know.
An angel that will let her lean on their shoulder
An angel that will protect her, an angel that will hold her
Dear Lord, send my friend Chelsea a fighter
An angel that will make her light shine brighter.

Lastly, Lord, I need the strongest angel you've got
An angel who doesn't need sleep, because he will be doing a lot
You see there's a guy and I need him to be safe
Because the love I have for him cannot be replaced.
Lord, please send a protector
An angel to also act as a deflector
Of anything negative that will cause him stress
Because honestly, Lord, he deserves the best
An angel to help him let his guard down
An angel that will always be around
To look out for him when he's all alone
And to watch over him while he walks home.
When I look at him I see my life
So Lord, tell that angel to protect him right
Because Montae is strong, as strong as they ever came
But Lord, even the strongest players need help in the game.

© Eduardo Hernandez

How We Live

I Am a Nomad

by Jaquelin Sanchez

I am a nomad
I wonder where I'll move next
I hear my parents whispering behind closed doors
I see my mom's dark, sunken eyes
I want to help, but I can't
I am a nomad

I pretend to be happy at school, as if nothing's wrong at home
I feel anguished when I have to move again
I touch the bare white walls as I leave
I worry if my parents can pay next month's rent
I cry because I'm exhausted
I am a nomad

I understand why we have to move for the thirteenth time
I say, "I'm fine," but I'm not
I dream of the day I won't have to pack anymore
I hope this next move will be our last
I am a nomad

Past Tense

by Nichole Landaverde

I was insatiable with your voice. Not because of the sound but what came out. You talked as if you were describing the world to a blind person, always with such great depth. The way your lips parted or the way your tongue touched the top of your mouth when speaking in Spanish. The way you spoke with great vocabulary or the way your mind was set. The way you talked when you were intensely passionate about something. The way you made every subject so appealing. You were never impassive with your facial expressions. But your appearance was not what attracted me. It was your mind. I was a sapiosexual towards you, my love.

You could see you had everybody mesmerized. The vibrations your tone allowed on my neck. The combination of words that had goosebumps all over my body. Your whisper was my undoing. You knew the effect you had on me. Everything was in slow motion near you. I embraced every moment, knowing nothing lasts forever. But I was brainless, naïve, so willing to even think twice. Your vibe was infectious. But you knew that.

Never Ending

by Anonymous

I feel as if I'm still being punished for his crime.

I was seven years old, a second-grader at Miramonte Elementary School in South East Los Angeles. My mom dropped my brother and me off every morning before school in the school's child-care facility. We also played there after school until she picked us up. I didn't mind staying until five or even six o'clock, for Miramonte Elementary felt like my second home.

A teacher, I'll call him Mr. Alexis, was new to the place. He was Mexican, in his late 30s, and he had a big, black bushy mustache. At first he seemed like a cool teacher. I thought of him as my second dad. In time Mr. Alexis became comfortable with the school and all the kids.

One afternoon after school my friend Brenda and I were reading a book in the library section of the school when Mr. Alexis suddenly grabbed my right arm and pulled me toward him. He placed me between his legs and grabbed my private part with his huge man hand. As he squeezed me, he let out soft moans. I begged Brenda to pull me away. She screamed, "Let her go!" and pulled me away. I sprinted to the restroom. I felt confused, physically hurt, and didn't know what to do.

For the next few days I avoided Mr. Alexis, terrified to go anywhere near him. He told my mom that I was ignoring him, as if he didn't know why.

One day after school in the child-care facility he threatened me. He said if I spoke out he would report my parents to immigration and my brother, sister, and I would be forced to live in foster care.

He touched me two more times. I didn't breathe a word. My mom noticed that my private part was red and asked if anyone had touched me. I said no. She said I could tell her anything, but I felt afraid, ashamed, and confused. Though even at age seven, I knew what he was doing was wrong.

A month passed before I worked up the courage to tell my mom. When I told her, I felt relieved, yet simultaneously felt more terrified than ever. My mom reported Mr. Alexis to someone at the school. A few other girls came forward and reported that he had also been inappropriately touching them.

Mr. Alexis was arrested.

Eventually he was convicted and sentenced to a 15-year prison sentence.

My mom sent me to a therapist. I hated going. Over a period of years I saw several therapists, and each one asked me the same questions:

"Where did he grab you?"

"How many times did this occur?"

And I would have to retell the same story over and over, in greater and greater detail. I felt as if I was being punished every time I repeated the story.

I spent the next six years in and out of therapy. I also had to appear in court and explain what happened in order to put Mr. Alexis behind bars. Sometimes the court sessions dragged on all day, and I hated being pulled out of school, away from my lessons and my friends, and driven downtown and hanging around the courthouse until I was called to the witness stand to testify.

I remember telling my mom, "This isn't fair. Why do I have to keep coming to court and repeating the same story they've heard before?"

My mom told me that this was how the justice system worked.

When it was all over I thought, "Thank you, God. No more repeating this ever again."

I locked these memories away, trying to forget what had happened to me as a child. I've worked hard to forget the pain and the crying and the on-going punishment of being victimized by a pedophile.

At the time I didn't notice, but I was no longer the same little girl I had been before the incidents. I began to hate school and all my teachers—not because they assigned me too much homework or because a few of them acted mean, but because of the incident that had happened so long ago.

Years later I learned that even before my abuse, Mr. Alexis' file had been red-flagged due to his actions at a previous school. And yet the Los Angeles Unified School District allowed him to work around children and to perpetuate the same crimes over and over again before he was apprehended.

Ten years have passed, and still I feel as if I am serving a life sentence of having to deal with shame.

Until this moment I have never told anyone except for therapists, lawyers, and judges, because this story is not something that is easy for me to say.

And yet now, sharing my story, I begin to feel a sense of relief. While writing these words, I cried and let out a lot of pain that I had been holding back for more than half my life. Writing this story has lifted a heavy weight off my body and soul.

I sense and I hope that this is my path to healing.

Unknown Feelings

by Miguel Gianfranco Guzman Valle

There is something inside of me
Emotions and feelings that I have never felt
But I hold them with a key
In a way to not let them break free.

My mind goes blank
And I don't know what to do with that
I know that this feeling isn't a prank
And is something that I always don't look at.

This life is too short for one to think clever
Keeping this feeling away is overwhelming me
Is something that I cannot lock up forever,
And I feel that it could come out like a sea.

In my life I have never felt like this
But this isn't something unknown to me
This feeling is cutting me in bits
And I know it will break free.

Inner Conflict

by Miguel Gianfranco Guzman Valle

Sometimes I just think
I think in the way I do things
If everything will relate and link
Connecting each think as a string

Just do what you think is right
And work in the way you know to do
Work until night
And do everything the day it's due

I think in myself in my mind
That sometimes I don't see that I am blind
And I think that my life is unkind
And that my life is already being timed

Don't over think and look for the best
Seek and work for what you want and need
So you will be able to progress
In a way that no one will know where it will lead

I learn and understand
And I know that I will stand
I will grab all my lessons and experiences with my hand
And I hope my mind will expand.

The Call

by Anthony Cortez

I was 16,234 days old when I answered my grandmother's telephone. The cold exterior of the telephone sent a shiver down my spine, reminding me of the night breeze, just like the nights my father and I would sit outside of my grandmother's house banging beats on the stone steps. It has been a long time since we have.

"Hello, who is this?" I said.

I looked down at my faded red shoes, dug in my toe, and kicked out some cereal left on the dining room floor.

"Would you accept a collect call from Eric Cortez?"

Are you joking? Arrested! I thought.

"No."

I could hear a faint voice behind the machine's message, my father's voice.

"I'm sorry, I'm so sorry." My father, calling from Corcoran State Prison.

I slammed down the telephone.

My father's been in and out of prison my whole life. He spent more time inside a prison than he has with me. Sadly, I have grown accustomed to a fatherless lifestyle.

Once off the telephone I sat down on my grandmother's gray juice-stained couch, rested my head against the armrest and thought, "Is this really happening?" He promised he was done. He promised her. He promised he wouldn't do this again.

I had spoken to my father the previous night. We sat outside talking about the basics—school, sports, and girls. But I had to ask the question that had been hanging over my head for so long. In a small raspy voice, throat dry as the Sahara Desert, I asked, "Dad, are you out of the gang for good?"

"Yes, why do you ask?"

"Well, that's my little sister inside, and I've grown up without a father. So did you, so you should know how much a child needs a father. You've left two children practically fatherless. So quit the damn gang and give your daughter the father I never had. This is your last shot to do right."

He turned to me, eyes glossy, head down, cheeks wet with tears. "Yes," he said.

"Good." I actually believed him. "Wow, please something, someone, watch over my father." We went back inside.

I walked into my baby sister's room. She lay on her pink blanket drinking her bottle. I lay next to her. She didn't move or cry. I turned my head toward the beautiful two-year-old.

"Dad's in jail again, so he's not going to be around much. I know you don't understand what I'm saying, but I hope you know this. I will always be here for you, no matter what the cost, no matter how big the fight. I love you."

When a father disappears, life reappears.

Empty Life

by Tyanni Gomez

That's all, I'm repeating in my head.
To get these stupid thoughts out of my head.

Have you ever lost someone? I have.
It's like, they were your freedom
As if they knew you, the real you.
Have you ever felt so lost without them? I have.
It's like, I'm sitting here in prison, crying, wondering, thinking …
As if that person accused you of something you haven't done.
Have you ever felt so locked in that you rethink this whole situation? I have.
As if concealing all your thoughts inside of you would help.

And …
It sucks because you want to be free again, but you can't because it's hard getting
out of this prison, because you're so guilty for what you've done, because you
want to know what made the monster in you.

And …
Then you think and realize you're just a human being with an empty mind, an
empty heart and just want an empty life.

I Am "Fifty Shade of F***** Up"

by Zaria Lampkins

I am "Fifty Shades of F***** Up"
I wonder how I became this way/why I'm this way
I hear people talk about me & not know my story
I see happy carefree people and I wish I was more like that
I want people to stop judging me before they get to know me

I am "Fifty Shades of F***** Up"
I pretend that I have nothing to hide
I feel little to no emotions
I touch? I don't. Because I don't like to be touched
I worry that things from my past will come back to haunt me
I cry ... I don't

I am "Fifty Shades of F***** Up"
I understand at times why I am the way that I am
I say I'm fine (ok, good, etcetera) when in reality I'm not
I dream nightmares in black and white
I try to see the good things in life
I hope my life will change or be changed by someone
I am "Fifty Shades of F***** Up"

Mom, Dad

by Randy Chavez

Mom, Dad
I have to tell you
some things that I haven't told
you. People might call it
ratting, but I call it
communication

My brothers would come home drunk
They are the ones who
gave me my first beer
We also went to our uncle's
ranch and fired some guns
They taught me the dealing business
I also went with them
to one of their dealing areas
Don't be mad or ashamed
that I've done this
I'm not going to fall for it

Remember that guy
I told you about that was
in the hospital?
Yeah, my brother was just
protecting their little brother
I will graduate high school
just like they did
But never give up
on me.

A Father's Betrayal

by Veronica Vargas

I hate my father's choices.
I can't wrap my mind around why he doesn't care.
Beer before his children.
He's consumed by it; it's who he is.
"I was born an alcoholic, an alcoholic I will die," he says.
It's engraved in my mind.
That drunk man who replaced my father.
His words slur, his eyes are bloodshot.
He's sitting in the dark, exhausted from the fight he had with my mom.
He calls for me.
"*Vero, ven.*" ("Vero, come.")
"*Que quieres?*" ("What do you want?"). Tears of anger burn my cheeks.
"*Ya no me quieres?*" ("You don't love me anymore?")
"*Ya me canse, ya no lo puedo hacer. Tu hijo ya tiene miedo que te van ha encontrar en la calle, muerto!*"
(I'm tired, I can't do this. Your own son is afraid they'll find you dead in the streets.")
He laughs.
I can smell the beer from where I stand.
I kneel at his feet.
My voice cracking.
I manage to get these words out.
"*Ya basta, por favor déjà de tomar!*" ("Just stop, please stop drinking!")
Silence so heavy it weighs me down, fills the room.
Until I hear him chuckle.
And within a blink of an eye, I had no father.
He became just a person, one who left a daughter, confused. Alone.
I don't get it.
I was Daddy's little girl.
Now I'm exhausted from fighting for him to change.
I give up.
Beer has possessed him.
While resentment and hurt have taken over my thoughts.
"I still love you," he says over the phone.
Then prove it, I repeat in my head.
Please.

Ashamed of Me

by Joslyn Stevenson

I feel like you're ashamed of me
Is it because I smoke trees
and get D's?
You'd say no,
but I know the truth
You think I won't make it
in this world
But just wait until I'm rockin' diamonds and pearls
with my master's degree
Ima G,
Didn't grow up in the streets,
but I came from a deadbeat family
Living with people who don't approve of me
takes a toll, but
Ima keep moving forward
because
that's what I want to do
Ima tired of feeling sorry for you,
like I was the one raised you
Ima be successful and prove it all to you.

Remember This

by Melissa Mateo

The monster from our dreams
He's real, but he can't hurt us anymore
He's gone, yet we still see him when we sleep
It's an unspoken rule between us
I know your story, yet you haven't spoken a word.
You're smiling, but I know you hurt.
We share the memories but not the pain.

Your heart didn't break the way mine did
Your eyes didn't see what I saw, and my eyes didn't see what you saw
Your ears didn't hear the screams
My ears didn't hear your "Stop, Dad, don't hit her, Dad, don't break
    that, Dad, I'm sorry, Dad" screams
But I know you screamed them, I know you cried those little eyes
    out and pulled the tears back when someone was near
Don't worry, honey; don't be scared, he's gone now.
But now that's the problem, he's gone.
I know you're better, that these nightmares are slowly fading
Slowly causing less harm as they travel back.
Remember this when you're feeling sad,
Remember this when the silence is too intense and the voices in your
    head won't stop,
Remember this when the flashbacks come back to haunt you,
Remember that you're not alone.
Remember that now when we scream, we wake up.

Disturbing the Peace

by De'Jon K. Jones

Was I an athlete headed to Vegas or a juvenile headed to jail?

I had been enjoying a peaceful sleep when suddenly I was jarred awake. I felt frightened and consciously slowed my breath so I could figure out what was going on. I maneuvered my way upstairs, peeking out window after window, following the noise as I gripped an aluminum baseball bat and hoped to alert my mom and sisters before the commotion around me actually presented itself.

We were being robbed, and as the man of the house I had no choice but to defend my family.

I heard a helicopter and voices yelling over a loudspeaker for us to come out.

The police were raiding us.

They kept shouting for my mom's boyfriend to come out first, otherwise they were going to come in and get him. My mom opened the front door. She exited the house. My sister followed and stood off to the side as demanded. As I approached the door I was met by the Special Ops Unit just like in a game of *Call of Duty*.

Each member held a flashlight and an automatic rifle from with a red beam aimed directly at my chest as I walked out with my hands up.

I looked into the dark skies and closed my eyes, afraid of what might happen next.

Then my mom's boyfriend appeared in the doorway.

The police aimed their red beam and their rifles at him.

He and I were corralled by a swarm of cops, snatched up, handcuffed and stuffed face first into a wall in a dark passageway along the side of our house. Guns were aimed at the backs of our heads.

When the unit command demanded that the weaponry be put down, a detective strolled over and filled us in on our situation.

The entire time he talked, all I could think about was my football team and how they'd be out looking for me if I didn't show up for school in a few hours. It was 5 a.m. and I was due to be in the parking lot adjacent to the Venice High School football field to travel to Las Vegas to play seven-man football. Instead I was standing in the cold morning air trembling in a tank top, boxers, and handcuffs.

Turned out I wasn't on my way to juvie hall, but neither was I on my way to play football. At that moment I was neither an athlete nor a criminal. I was a sixteen-year-old kid looking forward to celebrating his seventeenth birthday later that week.

I was released to my family and returned to my bedroom where I promptly fell asleep.

Three Decembers and a June

by Randy Chavez

December 2009.

My grandma passed.

I remember at the time I was playing MW2. My family and I were planning to leave for Mexico that night to visit her.

We did get to see her. But she was inside of her coffin.

That same December day was when I started to drink and hang with the wrong crowd.

I was ten years old.

December 2010.

My dad's birthday, Christmas, my grandpa's birthday. All fall on the same day.

I am told that my aunt went inside to give my grandpa his medicine.

"Call the doctor," I heard her scream. "He is not responding."

That's what woke me up.

My grandpa died on his birthday.

I drank three bottles of tequila.

Shot after shot.

June came around and my cousin introduced me to his AK-47.

Soon, I had held A's, .45s, .16s.

Just name it. I shot it.

I remember getting shot at. But I never got hit.

December 2011.

Some dudes screwed up.

My cousin sent people after them. But the dudes were never found. They left their house. For good.

I had witnessed drug deals. Big deals. Not $15 dollar deals.

In Mexico I carried my own strap because there are some snakes that would try to take my place. With my strap, I get respect and all I look for is respect. If you disrespect me I have this one person who will send people after you.

My family always wanted the best for me.

My parents always tell me and beg me to graduate.

But I don't know if one day I will get shot in Mexico and not come back to L.A. At least, not come back alive.

I promised myself I will stop drinking and hanging out with the wrong crowd.

I promised myself I will graduate in 2016 and make my family happy.

I Come From

by Kat Secaida

I come from having a police record, charged with battery
    and assault.
I am scared that I'm just like him.
Sometimes I can't control my anger.
I am scared that I'm just like him.
My father is in jail, again.
I am scared that I'm just like him.
He even went to court. Dad got community service.
I am scared that I'm just like him.

An inhaler installed in his car.
I've never seen him sober before.
Interesting Thanksgiving.
I've never seen him sober before.
It felt very different, everyone is clean.
I've never seen him sober before.
Flashbacks. I remember him drunk, and yelling.
I've never seen him sober before.

I don't want to be like my dad.
Locked up or dead.
My "friends" said I was uncontrollable, I don't remember.
Locked up or dead.
Happy I got arrested, it opened my eyes.
Locked up or dead.
Following his footsteps.
Locked up or dead.

I am scared I'm just like him.

Walked in Blind

by Nichole Landaverde

It was difficult to breathe for a bit. I guess all the stress and thinking became anxiety. Oftentimes I get anxiety attacks at any given moment. Thinking of my mother, even thinking of my father, made me feel stress. Not the situation itself, but the fact that I had made their problems my own. Most days I was locked up in my home. I felt like a prisoner.

My brother began to attend church, for my uncle is a pastor, but I felt isolated from the outside world. He kept insisting, trying to persuade me to join him, and I finally gave in.

First time walking in was frightening as hell. We were a few minutes late, but everyone had chosen their seats and were on their feet "praising the Lord." I felt all eyes on me, which I'm not fond of. Standing in front of an empty seat, feeling out of place. Feeling that I wasn't worthy of clapping or standing, for that matter. People there had grown up surrounded by nothing but church, but I was just out of the blue walking in. Of course I knew some people, as they had known me my whole life—being the pastor's niece and all. But the vibe this time is obviously different. They praise Him, cry to Him, let the whole week's worth of stress, anger, and even happiness out.

I couldn't pray or even cry. I couldn't feel what they felt towards Him. I was ashamed to be standing there, blind. I was ashamed that I couldn't connect, or feel passionate. It was my first time, and I knew it was understandable I was confused and lost, but I wanted to lose myself in the music, in the environment. That feeling made me go again.

Portrait of Mariana Hernandez, Kat Secaida & Nichole Landaverde © Hannah Schatzle

I Am

by Melissa Nava

I am a mommy's girl.
I wonder what my life would be without her.
I hear her say, "*Mi negrita te quire mucho carbona!*"
I see that her love for her kids is unconditional.
I want her to be by my side forever.

I am a mommy's girl.
I pretend to be an only child knowing that there are four of us.
I feel like the most wonderful/ghetto daughter she could have.
I touch her warm face and kiss her on her cheek.
I worry that one day I will lose my mom due to kidney failure.
I cry when she ends up in the hospital.

I am a mommy's girl.
I understand that one day my mom will not be there to save me from all
my bad actions.
I say, "I love you too much *un chinga*."
I dream that one day I can donate my kidney to her so we can both live a
wonderful life together.
I try to have a positive attitude towards anything I do and accomplish.
I hope to keep my mom with me through my ups and downs.
I am a mommy's girl.

To Wake up Alone

by D. Leigh

To wake up alone is to wake up exposed.

Exposed to danger and vulnerability.

Vulnerable to harm, vulnerable to fear.

Fear that gives me nightmares, fear that provides unshed tears.

To wake up alone and see no one around, makes you hear creeks and sounds
That didn't exist before now.

To wake up with no mom, no dad, no uncle to protect you, makes you
independent, resentful and neglected.

To wake up alone bleeding from your nose and coughing it from your mouth
makes you scared, scared like a child running from a hound.
Blood, blood, and more bloodshed mixed with tears are now soaked in my bed.

To wake up alone and have no brother or sister as guide makes you a thrill seeker,
wanting to ride every ride.

To wake up alone and feel empty inside is a pain that has no bounds.

To wake up alone screaming for help, and to realize no one's coming and you're by
yourself. Makes waking up alone every day after that, to face every day and see
facts as facts.

Life as an Addict

by Luis Fajardo

I didn't realize I was an addict until I attended a POPS meeting. POPS stands for Pain of the Prison System. It's a club that meets on Wednesday at Venice High. It was my first time attending and a guest speaker, Khanisha Foster, talked about her experiences living with addicted parents.

That's when I realized I was an addict.

As far back as I can remember someone in front of me had used a type of drug. Living in a mostly Hispanic neighborhood in East Hollywood, drugs were in everybody's hands. As a 10-year-old boy I knew very little, but I watched, listened, and caught on.

My sister was 15, hanging out with gang members and shooting crystal meth up her nose while our mom was in the next room. I would sit against the door in case my mom came in so my sister had enough time to hide the magazine filled with white rocks. All the while I pretended to play in front of the door.

I feel partially to blame for my sister's addiction. I lied for her many times. And I would stay awake till after midnight to let my sister in the house without our mom finding out.

Eventually my sister was caught using.

After going away for three months, she was sent away and we could not see nor hear from her for six months. I felt horrible because now I was smoking on my own and telling myself I would be different and never be an addict.

Now, seven years later, I'm following in almost the same footsteps. Not to the same degree, but I have been cited, failed classes, and lost my mom's trust and love, all because of weed.

I don't want to see my mom hurt like she was hurt when my sister was sent away.

My mom hugged me while crying, "Please *mijo*, don't be like your sister. Be someone in life."

I can't let her down.

Absent

by Angel Guerrero

My name is Angel Guerrero, President of POPS the Club, and here is my story. My father, Raul Guerrero, has been absent from my life since I was just over one; to be frank, he wasn't there at all. He left a black hole in me that was littered with anger, sadness, bitterness, and so many questions.

Many people don't understand the hardships of not having a father, so let me show you. Many years ago, my mother was driving around in Compton on a nice day with my siblings and me. A nice day, mind you, until my brother and sister asked my mom where their father was. "He left because he doesn't love you," my mother said. The look on their faces is still difficult to describe: These two naïve and innocent little faces having trouble comprehending how their father could not love them, want to be with them. Sometimes I ask myself the same thing. "Why?" Many years later, I ask myself the same question. "Why?"

That question may never be answered. I will not be the last, nor am I the first to ask. These same questions that I continue to ask myself may never find answers. And that is why, in my heart where my father ought to be, there is a black hole littered with anger, sadness, bitterness, and so many questions, never to be healed, never to be put away in peace.

Portrait of Angel Guerrero © Hannah Schatzle

Let the Music Take Me Away

by Nelvia Marin

The day I was waiting for is around the corner—January 15. Wake up at 9:30, no need for an alarm clock because my personal alarm clock is as bright as the stars in the solar system. Hop into a warm bath, fill the tub halfway and softly pour in sea salt. Smell the aroma of Brazilian rosewood. Get the chills before I get used to the water. Lie there to relieve the butterflies in my stomach. Like always I'm nervous. Nothing new.

Hop out and quickly dry myself. Dress myself, make a delicious breakfast—the usual, Frosted Flakes with almond milk and half a cup of apple juice. While I eat I look at my clock—rusted metal with faded Roman numerals. Time is going slowly by. Big hand on the 11, and my phone rings. Brittany.

Walking out the redwood door wearing a striped muscle tank paired with black sweats and black Adidas, typical hip-hop look. Hoping to fit in, I speed-walk my way to the car. I introduce myself and hop in the backseat of a 2007 all-white Wrangler Jeep. On our way to Westwood.

Takes a while. You know LA's a slow city.

Arriving, walking into the mid-sized studio, my butterflies return. Four mirrors. If you look left there is one, right another, behind me another and in front of me a fourth Dream dance studio. Waxed wood floors with that perfect grip. AC to keep the studio cool.

The music system plays "Toot It and Boot It," by YG.

Brittany moving her head, then her hands, and now her feet. She already has our choreography. Forming a triangle, shortest to tallest. Copying Brittany's reflection in the mirror. Keeping up is my problem.

Too much stomping feet and popping out our chests, my body just can't keep up. But I continue even though I look like a red pepper because of how embarrassed I am.

Brittany shouts, "That's it for today, ladies."

I drop on my back to the cold floor to catch some air.

When I go home that night I do a couple of crunches and jumping jacks because I feel out of shape.

I'm a hip-hop dancer on the weekends.

My Cousin Alberto

by Melanie Becerra

My cousin Alberto had been a drug addict since he was 15. He lived with my family and me for as far back as I can remember. Alberto came from Mexico when he was 14 in hopes that the United States would bring him better opportunities. As soon as he arrived, he started to experiment with drugs. Marijuana, cocaine, and even meth. Throughout my childhood I saw him transform from a young boy into a scary adult. He had been a sweet boy with a chubby face, full of life. But after years of drug abuse his face held a sinister stare. It was long and skinny, and his eyes were sunken so deep that they looked black.

Alberto started to act weird. He'd talk to himself, and he experienced extreme mood changes. He was diagnosed as schizophrenic and bipolar, both caused by his constant drug abuse. My parents were terrified of Alberto, but they never had the heart to kick him out. We were the only family members he had. My parents hoped that he'd never harm my siblings or me. But they could only do so much to protect us.

In the summer of 2011, Alberto finally snapped.

It was just days before I started high school. I was 14. I was out with friends at the local park. My friends and I were hanging out on the grass when I received a call from my brother.

"Where are you? Are you okay?" he asked.

"I'm fine," I said. "What's wrong?"

"Just come home. Now."

I ran home having no idea of what could have happened. As I approached my house, I saw three cops and an ambulance.

I saw my brother and ran to him and asked, "What happened? Please tell me everyone is okay!"

"It's Alberto," my brother said. "He tried to kill me."

They were both in the kitchen. Alberto pulled a knife out of the cabinet and charged at him. My mother saw Alberto running at my brother and tried to fight him off. She screamed for help. My dad and neighbors came. It took four men to pull Alberto off of my brother and mother.

I couldn't believe what I was hearing.

Alberto went to jail. He told the judges he didn't do anything and that he had no reason to be in jail. I hated hearing that. After he tried to kill my brother, he denied it had ever happened. He deserved to be locked up.

Alberto often wrote to me. He'd draw me pictures and tell me about his life inside. He'd tell me about the friends he made and the things they thought of him. One of the friends he made is an artist and was teaching Alberto to draw.

But I never wrote back. I didn't visit him. I didn't want to see him. I didn't know

My Prison

by Tyanni Gomez

I'm in prison
I'm locked in.
I'm concealing.
Not feeling.
I'm lost.
I'm alone
And I'm afraid.

I stare at the wall, and all I see is nothing.
I stare to my left ... nothing.
I stare to my right ... nothing.

Silence is all I hear.
Silence has taken me over.
Silence made me who I am.
Silence is my way of thinking of the past.

Thinking ... about the past.
Thinking ... about my smile, where it used to shine ... like stars.
Thinking about it more and more.
Deeper and deeper
    And ...
    There ...
    I shatter ... in pain ... wishing
    I wasn't locking up this pain inside me.

Two Shots

by Julissa Vega

Two shots of hate from a mouth as loud as a gun
Like an assassin
Who does it for fun?
Two deafening blows from a war that had just begun
Life gone away
I'm done

Two red roses resting on a casket
The wind blows
Leaving only one
The world disappears
Like the setting sun

Dad's Last Day

by Jaquelin Sanchez

I woke around 2:30 a.m. to the sounds of my parents screaming at each other behind their bedroom door. I slid out of bed to see what their fighting was about.

When I opened their door I saw my mom on the far side of the bed and my dad near the door. I smelled alcohol on his breath. I asked him to quiet down so I could sleep, but he ignored me and continued his tirade at my mom. He wanted money to go out and buy beer.

"Would you please shut up and leave my mom alone?" I said, and I grabbed my mom by the arm and led her into my sisters' bedroom. My dad stumbled along behind us.

By now my sisters had woken up, and I took my youngest sister, Kimbo, to the living room to calm her down. She was crying and calling for my mom.

Magali stayed with me to help keep my dad away from my mom. He tried coming after her, but I intervened.

My mom told me to call the cops. So I ran to the phone. I was shaking and mistakenly dialed 9911. A police dispatcher picked up, but before I could say a word my dad yanked the phone from me and flung it at the couch. Then he started toward my mom. She ran out the door and into the street. A moment later my dad chased after her. And then Margali ran after them both.

I stayed inside with Kimbo.

The phone rang. The police. I told them what was going on.

They told me they were on their way.

Before they hung up I said, "And bring the paramedics," for at that moment my mom returned with Magali. She closed the door and locked it. My eye instinctively moved to my mother's knee. Blood.

"What happened?" I asked.

"He pushed me to the sidewalk."

We waited for the police. My mother filed a report.

My dad never came back.

Why I Couldn't Leave

by Nicole Landaverde

See him twice a month or so,
Knowing it could end anytime,
Knowing I could tell someone what he does,
But not wanting to bring up the past.
Knowing I'm already too late.
He is dangerous to himself and everyone around.
But I was at the point where dangerous did not scare me.

He spoke as if he were twenty years older. His eyes were dilated as if he took drugs. His breath smelled of nothing but alcohol, not even his scent. He stepped close, closing the gap in between. I was no longer inhaling fresh air. I froze, not knowing what his intentions were. I held his stare, wanting to help him, but also afraid of which person would come out.

He yelled his lungs out and once he began to sink down, I was no longer afraid. He needed help, help I wanted to give. Tears fell from his eyes, kneeling down, I kneeled next to him. I felt no fear. Thanking God I did not meet his rage side. He looked so vulnerable. All I wanted to do was cry by his side, but what's worse than a person crying? Two people crying. I couldn't help if I forced myself to feel as down as he looked. No talking, just the movement of his shoulders shaking. We were sitting on the floor like statues. I couldn't relate. I couldn't understand what he was going through, but I couldn't leave him alone.

He Deserves to Live

by Veronica Vargas

This is what I know today—my Uncle Jose is finally being treated right.
As a human.

He's not from here. He came from Zacatecas when he was young.
He has no insurance.
His failing kidneys didn't seem to matter.
Took five diabetic attacks before a doctor even glanced at him.
It didn't matter that he's a dad or a father figure to me, his niece.
No money—they overlook you.
No insurance—you might as well be invisible.

I remember the day before my uncle's operation.
They were going to move the tubes for his dialysis treatment into his arm.
The left arm just like his mom had it.
I could see the fear masked behind his eyes.
He tried to keep it together but I could tell he was falling apart.

His eyes are now swallowed by dark around them.
His once tanned skin is now pale and colorless.
And although he laughs, I can hear the breaths of pain hidden between those
    moments of joy.

He woke.
Weeks had passed.
Now he has a longer chance of raising his kids, of seeing them grow up.
My Uncle Jose deserves to live.
Dialysis.
Every Monday, Wednesday, and Friday.
He'll be okay.
I hope.
As long as they see him still.
As long as they view him as human.
Actually, as long as they can turn a profit.

Because They Are Family

by Randy Chavez

What I heard
what you had said
when you came back from that party
you were shocked
the door of our house was opened
you asked mom, but she didn't know,
she had been with you all night
you went inside, turned on the lights
everything was upside down
you looked for the .44
under the couch
it wasn't there
went to the backroom to look for the 9
it wasn't there
you went to your room to look for the M16
it wasn't there
you knew if you checked the other
2 rooms
the other guns weren't going to be there
you went into the storage room
and got the other 9
then ran to the front of the house
then down the block,
you didn't realize that
the truck that was speeding down the street
was the one who went in and stole half
of your stuff
after a few days you knew who it was
because they are family
you found some stuff in our backyard
and in the neighbor's backyard,
but
you knew the neighbors weren't the ones.

Where We Stand

© Victor L.M. Demic

Where Do I Stand?

by Daisy Lopez

I enter the world not knowing who I am and where I am.

My mom holding me tight, feeling the love of a mother.

Opening my eyes, not knowing what I'm looking at.

First words, Mama, Papa. Not even able to understand what they mean.

Taking my first step, feeling strong.

Family members holding me, telling me I'm cute and adorable but not able to know how to take a compliment.

Very stubborn.

At home lying down and hearing people argue. In my head: What is going on? Too little even to understand.

Step by step, years pass by, and I continue to grow and am finally able to understand more.

Waking up one morning to a loud banging, late night, my parents run downstairs, cops outside, looking up to my sister Bianca whose tears are dropping to her gown.

In my head: What's going on?

My brother, Jordan, sleeping in his room.

Cops run upstairs straight to my brother's room. Take my brother. Crying, wondering what is going on, why are they taking him?

Too young even to understand.

Living my life wondering: Where's my brother?

Going to school, being a troublemaker, always trying to figure out: Why am I being so bad? Is it from the anger of not having my brother around? Is it from the lies they keep telling me?

A couple of months pass by, and my brother finally comes home.

Never home, always out. Looking at my mom tearing up. Not knowing what's going on. My brother is never around. Why? I ask my mom. No answer. I ask my dad, again no answer. I ask my sister Cindy, again no answer. I ask Bianca, and again no answer.

Years pass by. Bianca and I go to first communion every Tuesday after school. Mom isn't able to pick us up so she asks my brother to pick us up. Stay after school waiting on my brother, who doesn't show up.

The day I see my godmother and she says, "Let's go." I look at her and say, "No, Jordan is picking me up." She says, "I know, but something happened."

We go straight to her house. Sitting there, lost, not knowing what's going on. My parents show up hours later. Bianca shows up.

Asking "What's going on?" No response.

Confused, heart beating really fast. In the background all I hear is the sounds of cops everywhere, from Cattaraugus to National. Blocked the whole street. Helicopters roaming everywhere.

Hours pass. We go home and the house looks a mess. And my brother, Jordan, is gone.

I ask, "Why is it so messy?"

All they say is, "The cops were searching for something. And they took your brother."

My entire life I wonder where my brother is. I wonder why is my life so confusing. Years later, I am able to ask my mom why my brother isn't around.

She finally told me. He was a witness to an attempted murder. I still didn't understand what that meant, but my sister was able to explain it to me.   A   t times I think: Who's my brother? Why is he in jail? Why don't I have a single memory with him?

I question myself all the time. I was just too little to understand anything. Never had a brother-and-sister bond with him.

To this day I don't know what is going on. I cry myself to sleep. My anger is so strong that I do things I don't want to do. I don't blame my brother for my anger, I just blame him for not being a brother. There might times when I take the exact steps that my brother took just so I can feel a lot closer to him.

My life has been rough. I live in a house with both parents and all my siblings. My mom always gets me in trouble, always yelling at me, always trying to argue. My dad always hitting me for no reason. If Bianca does something bad, I get in trouble for it and he hits me. I'm always arguing with Bianca, always fighting. And Cindy? If it ain't about her daughter, it's about food, always fighting and arguing. I might sometime cause these messes, but I don't mean to. I love my family just as much as I love food.

It's just with the family that I have I feel left out of the picture.

I always wear a smile. I'm always hyper happy and turning up (as they say nowadays). Everyone always thinks I'm just one happy person, but in reality, behind this happy smiling face, I'm dealing with a lot of stuff. I've been through a lot, and no one understands, not even my family. I act the way I act for many reasons.

My entire life, since I was little, I heard that I was adopted or found behind a dumpster. Yeah, I mean I know sometimes we joke around and say things like that, but constantly saying it messed with my head, and my mom went along with it.

So it's more about not feeling loved and not having a family who was there or talked to me, asking, "What's wrong?"

I love my family very much, and they think I don't, but that's fine.

They just don't understand: I'm just a teenager in a world full of people, looking for myself and finding out where I stand.

I Am the Fetus of an Affair

by Elia Guadalupe Espinosa

I am the fetus of an affair
I wonder how long it would have taken mother to tell me, before I found
   out from someone else. I hear a heart beating
I see almond eyes staring into a brown-skinned oval-shaped woman
I want to know who I am
I am the fetus of an affair
I pretend I know who I am, the child who came from Mother
I feel madness, because I grew up hearing that I looked like Father, a man I
   never knew, but a man that I look so much like
I touch my long fingers as mother says, "You have your father's fingers."
   Who is Father? Who am I?
I worry I will never know who I am
I cry myself to sleep every night, wondering if one day he'll pass by. Just a
   glimpse is all I need.
I am the fetus of an affair
I understand my father never wanted me, that is why he left.
I say, "Screw him," I didn't need him anyway
I dream of marrying a man who could be father to my children, the father
   I never had.
I try to close my eyes so I won't see the man who left me behind
I hope to be twice as good a mother as the one I had
I am the fetus of an affair.

There Are Four

By Irvin Gutierrez-Lopez

There are four.
The center of the hallway in the West Building 2nd floor.
Once the bell rang for lunch or nutrition, that's where we were.
Keivan, Chris, William, and myself.
It was our spot and no one could take it from us.

Four friends always hanging out
Always talking and never with a new crowd.
People always wondered why we always hung out.
It's because we always had each other's back when we had our
    ups and downs.
There are four.

They were the coolest friends I ever had.
Until one day it all went bad
Because now they've graduated and I stayed back.
Now the spot is empty, no one is there, there is one.

Pigs

by Kei-Arri McGruder

What's the point of learning all those fancy moves
if all you do
is pull out your gun
when you feel somebody is a threat to you
even if they have no weapon.
Just because they do not obey you
does not give you the right to shoot.
We give too much control over to so many
of such little strength
and that's
where things need to change.

A Child of God

by Kei-Arri McGruder

I have no race I am a child of god
But I have opinions on the way I live and
The world around me
All the black people getting beat in
The early days that seemed unfair to
Me, but now that we are free
We misuse our freedom to look as
Dumb and stupid as our ancestors used to be
We have great opportunities and
We misuse these things like that
Beat you and torture you when they
Say go to school. Today we act as if
We are at the place in the world we
Wanna be pants all hanging in the ghetto
Slanging and shooting each other, gang banging
This is sad to see what we have come to be
What happened to black power
To the people not just blacks but blacks
Whites yellow all the people but I can
Only worry about one group at a time
And we wonder why they stereotype us
Look at what we have come to be
Martin Luther King. All the great
Leaders to help us get as free
As we can be would be disappointed by what
They see. We wonder why people don't wanna
Be around us, be in school with us.
We run around like fools. We worship
The fools who kill people steal dreams
Bring you into your own death
We need to make a difference in the way we carry ourselves as a
     whole
Accomplish greater goals rather than
High school graduate. Try to become a college graduate with a
     Master's degree
Then under achieve
That just makes you think I don't see how hard that is/but to me
We have let down the dream

I Am Not Easily Labeled

by Jeannie Cajas

I am not easily labeled
I wonder why things are the way they are
I hear people mocking me
I see those who said they cared turn away
I want to be a better version of me

I am not easily labeled
I pretend to be full of smiles, but I am not full of life
I see the weight ready to be lifted off my shoulders
I touch my uneven skin
I worry about not connecting with others
I cry at inappropriate times

I am not easily labeled
I understand most people's ideas and opinions
I say "labels are for cans"
I dream of a better tomorrow

I try to be considerate
I hope no one person is an exact definition
I am not easily labeled

I Am Useless

by Leo Cruz

I am useless
I wonder if I am ever going to change and actually be good
   for something.
I hear everyone talking about their futures in college
I see everyone getting ready to graduate
I want to graduate
I am useless
I pretend to ignore it, act like there is nothing wrong
I feel ashamed of myself
I touch the very bottom of the abyss
That's how low my life is
I worry that I am going to lose everything
I cry inside so no one can see
the weak side of me, not even myself
I am useless
I understand that I don't do anything to change this but
   that's because I don't know where to start
I say to myself, "Maybe one day I'll change"
I dream that one day I'll be different
I'll be worth something
I try so hard to get myself up all alone
I hope that one day I can change
Be something else, someone worthwhile, but for now
I am useless

Because of You

by Dannie Maddox

I was raised around alcoholics, druggies, and violence. I was taught how to become violent when someone tries to control me or walk over me. I was raised around gang members and criminals. From the time I was six, they were teaching me how to defend and to protect myself at all times. My family lived by this motto: "The streets don't make or break you, they show you the real & the fake." I have loved ones in jail because they thought the streets could make them and loved ones who the street broke because of the fake ones.

My family believes in honesty, loyalty, and respect. Ever since I was eight, I was the biggest crybaby in the family because I didn't want to do things that everyone else was doing. I didn't want to fight or steal. They called me scary, crybaby, and momma's baby. I allowed them to call me that because I was afraid to defend myself.

My older cousins realized I wasn't living up to my family's motto: "Honestly, loyalty and respect," so they put through a lot of challenges. They bullied me at home, and I was getting bullied at school. I was afraid to go to school or family gatherings. All I wanted to do was stay in my room, locked up. My mom noticed that I was gaining weight, coming home unhappy, and that I wasn't talking about my day or the times I spent with my "friends" because I didn't really have any.

In my sixth-grade year, my mom sat me down for a talk. She asked me why was distancing myself from school and family. I hung out with just two of my cousins; I didn't like the rest of them. My mom signed me into Audubon Middle School, where I got into fights. She threatened to kick me out of the house and send me to Vegas if I didn't change my attitude. I was living in my family's motto.

So I decided to change my attitude and my personality. I changed schools because I felt that would help me start a positive future. I joined softball so I wouldn't have to think about the negative aspects of my life. I met Michaela Richards and felt like she was the only one who could relate to my pain. I built a friendship with her in and out of school. I wanted to have a real friendship with her because she wasn't fake.

In eighth grade I stopped playing softball because I felt like I had someone to hang out with and have fun with. I felt like I wasn't alone, like I could actually be myself around Michaela and a few others. I wasn't afraid to defend myself or talk to others or to have a big group of friends. I felt like I was different person until I found out who my real friends were and who my fake ones were.

I started school with ten friends at the beginning of my eighth-grade year, and I left with just two. I didn't understand what had happened, but I knew things happened for a reason, and I thought of my family's motto: "The streets don't make or break you, they just show you the real & the fake." I finally understood what that meant.

My ninth-grade year I was alone. I started a new school and wanted to find new friends. I felt like Michaela and I weren't going to be friends anymore, but I still want to find a new best friend. I wanted to join softball, but my mom wanted me to join cheer. I was kind of hurt when the cheer coach told me I couldn't do two sports at a time. It was either cheerleading or nothing, so I became a cheerleader for my mother's sake and because I hoped I would enjoy it the way I had enjoyed softball.

When I moved to Manual Arts High School in tenth grade, I quit cheer and joined the softball team. I started as centerfielder, even though I was in junior varsity. It felt good to play the game again. The girls I played with were more than just other females. They became family. We spent hours on the field, laughing, crying, hurting, being frustrated, yelling at each other and being happy. I had never felt so complete until I became varsity catcher. Never before had I felt so complete and happy as I did when I reconnected with this sport.

Yes I have friends, yes I have family, but there is nothing better than playing the sport I love.

And when I am on the softball field, I am home.

When We Dream

© Eduardo Hernandez

The Day

by Anthony Cortez

I am not certain what day it was, but on this day my life changed. I walked into my first period class at 8:05 a.m. As usual I was five minutes late. I sat down trying not to call attention to myself. I opened *Tuesdays with Morrie*, the book I had been reading for the past few weeks. Soon I became distracted by my thoughts of my friend Tegan. She was on vacation in Virginia. I imagined Tegan with her short black hair hanging barely over her soft hazel eyes, sitting in front of her Apple laptop watching an anime show called *Sailor Moon*.

Soon sunlight peeked through the windows and illuminated the room. Classmates who sat near me started to whine.

"The light is too bright, I hate it," they said in annoying, high-pitched voices that irritated me.

To pass the time I began writing about my sorrow and depression. Every few minutes I looked around the light blue room, listening to my classmates' pencils and pens as they glided along their pages. I thought about what they were thinking and how they felt. I wondered if any of my classmates could see how engulfed in sadness I was.

Near the end of the class period, Mr. Danziger stood strong and confident at his tan-colored podium and spoke to the class. My mind drifted off to another world as he began to speak. I stared at the tree outside the classroom window. I pondered how easy it must be to be a tree—all it has to do is consume water, sunlight, and nutrients. A tree's life is simple; it grows and dies. I envied the tree.

When I stopped daydreaming, my attention fell upon my classmates. They were smiling, chatting with one another as they were collecting their belongings and getting ready to leave class. Mr. Danziger's deep voice broke my attention.

"Anthony, talk to me after class," he said.

"Okay," I said. What would he want to talk to me about, I wondered? I turned my work in on time.

The bell rang, alerting students to go to second period. I stood and walked a few steps and stood beside Mr. Danziger.

I am not certain of his exact words, but he said something like, "Your essay was good. You're a great writer. Next semester come to class more." He held out his hand for me to shake.

"Thank you," I said in a quiet voice. I gripped his hand. I could feel his smooth, warm palm against my own.

At that moment I felt stunned, filled with disbelief. I have always believed I was nothing special and no one actually noticed me. But at that moment I felt different. For the first time I didn't feel like an outcast. I felt as if I actually had something special to offer the world.

Shaking Mr. Danziger's hand filled me with gratitude, an empowering feeling that made me feel like I could accomplish anything as long as I put my mind, heart, and soul into it.

Mom and Me

by Ia'Leah Cain

1. I remember when my mom was incarcerated. I was six years old and I was living with my grandma
2. I remember when she called and told me she loved me, but I didn't understand why she wasn't there
3. I remember when I cried every night wishing she would come home
4. I remember when she came home I was so happy I couldn't believe it
5. I remember when she went back to prison. I was 12 years old.
6. I remember when people used to ask me, "Where's your mom," and I used to say she was on vacation.
7. I remember my mom being in and out of my life.
8. And sometimes I remember when she was home.
9. I remember when I watched my dad die when I was six.
10. I remember how sad I was, and how I was mad at everyone.
11. I remember when I sat in the courtroom to testify.
12. I remember looking at the boys who murdered my dad.
13. I remember when the judge said "27 years to life."
14. I remember waking up with my dad next to me.
15. I remember dreaming about him.
16. But then I remember, it's all just a dream.

My Secret Life

by Marianne Valencia

The Secret Life of Bees, by Sue Monk Kidd, turned me on to literature.

I read it twice during my sophomore year, and both times I read it from cover to cover in one day, a totally new experience for me.

I loved this book's flow; it made me feel as if I were jumping into the surf and riding a long, smooth wave punctuated by occasional sudden and unexpected turbulence. When I finished reading I longed to read everything Ms. Kidd had written.

The Secret Life of Bees changed me in a way I had not expected. Since reading the novel I have begun reading more and more novels and watching fewer and fewer movies. I've been shocked to find how easy it is now to turn off the TV, or not to turn it on at all. I'd rather read.

All the books I have picked up since *The Secret Life of Bees* have not disappointed. Maybe that's because now when I read I find myself in a relaxed, meditative state of mind. I read, breathe deeply, and fall into the story. I quickly learned that every author has his or her own rhythm, own meter, own musical approach to language. And after reading *The Secret Life of Bees* I was able to begin seeing the world the author created rather than just hearing her words in my mind. I feel as if I am a witness to every moment. Perhaps I now see novels as films, which is why I no longer feel the pull to watch.

My connection to *The Secret Life of Bees* was deepened by my connection to its characters. I felt a bond with them, with their deepest thoughts, their hidden emotions and how they met obstacles, struggled to overcome them, and changed throughout the story. These characters' strengths gave me the hope that I can, throughout my life, make meaningful changes as well.

When I sat down to read *The Secret Life of Bees* I expected it to be just another school assignment, a number of pages to work my way through until the end. I did not expect this novel to change the way I viewed reading. I did not expect it to change my life for the better. But it did.

For that I will always be grateful, and for that I will continue to read and read and read.

Thoughts

by Miguel Gianfranco Guzman Valle

Hate and Love
That is a feeling that seems to be a myth
But that is something no one can escape from
No matter where you are, no matter whom you are with

Life and Death
Similar to love and hate
Indistinguishable from each other
The way one expresses is the way one seeks after many others

Peace and War
Have in their hand the secret to bring death to life
Make things that everyone thinks is all right
When other people strive

Give and Take
Wars give people hate and take peoples' lives
But peace brings people love and takes peoples' hate.
That is the world people await

Theme for English B

by Elia Guadalupe Espinosa
(based on a poem by Langston Hughes)

The instructor said,
go home and write
a page tonight
and let that page come out of you
then it will be true.
15, oval-shaped-faced, almond-eyed, brown-skinned Hispanic girl
At home I'm considered the lazy no good.
She always says, "You sit there doing what? Nothing while I'm here cleaning up."
I don't exactly just sit, if she only knew what I am doing.
Every day after school, I grab my journal and start writing.
I space into a marvelous world of no worries, no screaming, no demanding, just
    my mind and my journal. These pages contain my history, my biography, and
    she asks, "What are you doing?"
I write my life
June 20, 1997. 7:45 p.m.
I was born that late night in Perla Hospital in Mexico, DF, birth seemed perfect.
    Everything seemed perfect.
She'd always say the first thing she saw were those light brown, marble-shaped
    eyes staring right into her.
Papa wasn't there. He still isn't. He left before I was born.
I grew up with a good image of Mama.
Just before I entered my teens, things started to change—my mind, my body. I
    felt like my body was being invaded by a maniac diva.
It was never easy to collaborate with Mama.
We'd argue every day, over every single thing I did.
She only believed in right, her own meaning of right, to be like her, a strong,
    hardworking, independent, responsible woman.
I was 13, dependent. I had no other shoulder to cry on. No other hand to hold.
I knew she wanted me to be responsible, but I couldn't do it all alone. I've been
    afraid all my life of letting go. She will never understand that.
Never.

A Prayer for Peace

by Erika Fernandez

I pray for everyone to get along. To end racism. To end violence and to put down their weapons.

The world is a beautiful thing that we have; humans have no right to destroy it.

I pray that there are no more wars between countries and that there is an end to gang violence—it takes away too many innocent lives.

I pray for people to learn to forgive and to avoid turning their hatred inward. To learn that everyone makes mistakes and deserves a second chance.

I pray that people will accept each other no matter their external differences and to understand that every life matters.

I pray for all humans to unite and help each other and to be friendly to everyone.

I pray for people to love themselves for who they are and to embrace that.

For all these things I pray.

And above all, I pray for peace.

Revealed

by Veronica Vargas

I found an escape through word-filled pages.

I sat for hours on the corner of the couch lost in the world of Dave Pelzer's writing. Little did I know that *A Child Called It* would spark my interest in literature. At age 13 I didn't even know such a craving could exist.

Here I was, barely a teenager, who thought her life was a total mess. Never did it cross my mind that someone out there, some stranger, had it worse.

All that was visible to me was that I was the daughter of an alcoholic who was in and out of my life and a mom who was always ill.

As I read this memoir, a simple book really, I became oblivious to my teenage angst.

How had I not known; how had I not noticed that others suffered too?

Here was a boy beaten, abused, tortured by his own mother. Abandoned by his father. Yet he overcame all these physical and psychological wounds and found forgiveness.

Pelzer's book left me in awe of how pain can be healed, how literature can fuel the healing process. I found myself reading more and more books. All genres were welcome.

This memoir made me realize that no matter how bad or alone I might feel, there is always someone out there experiencing the same or worse and that I can struggle to overcome the horrific. And that finding forgiveness can be the key to freedom.

A Child Called It, though a simply told story, altered my view of the world, changed my perspective on every aspect of life. This book expanded my mind, helped my heart grow, and left me craving more books to read, more lives to explore. I wanted to lose myself in a thousand authors' stories.

Pelzer spoke to me directly, telling me that there was so much more beyond the world of my overcrowded public-school classrooms and the often mean streets of my section of LA.

I was fortunate to have discovered the love of literature in seventh grade. It sneaked up on me unexpectedly, as all good books sneak up on the reader and pull them into their secret worlds.

My love of literature is the gift that I will hold close throughout my life.

Nothing Too Special

By Kei-Arri McGruder

I have no real interest in Venice High School
   The only reason I come here is to get
   Away from the hellhole I call home.
All the yelling, all the screaming most of the time
   Makes me wanna just run away and leave
I stay to myself, trying to make it through another day
I don't like people in my face, so please don't
Try to be all friendly with me, because you will be wasting your time.
   And sooner or later you will just end up
   Leaving me.
   I don't say much and I barely like talking
   To people, so you will just get bored with me, sadly.
The only place I really enjoy being is on the wide-open space
Of the track and field
I enjoy passing time there, playing soccer
On the field with big mud holes and yellow grass.
I also like to get on the track,
Throw on my spikes and practice my figures
For my next meet, trying to stay unaffected.
And sometimes I just like walking around
The track playing my music, wishing I
Could lay a blanket down and kick back
   Let all my pain go away as I watch
   The clouds and close my eyes
   And hope to see another day.

How I Learned to Make Japanese Rice Balls

by Brittany Weight

Standing at the omusubi station with my boss ...

Keiko: First you take roughly a palm-sized amount of rice. Then you take two scoops of beef and press it into the rice. You got it?

Brittany: Yeah, even though my hands burn a little, what's next?

Keiko: Now you take the CP10, twist it, and start shaping the rice into a triangle, but leave it kind of chunky so it doesn't fall over.

Brittany: How do I shape it?

Keiko: Make both of your hands into a cup shape and place the rice in between, then gently squeeze. Keep flipping it so you get all sides equally. Then ta-da! You have an omusubi.

Brittany: I don't think I'm doing this right, am I?

Keiko: You're doing fine, it doesn't look bad, just squeeze a little harder.

Brittany: Like this?

Keiko: Yup! Great progress, Brittany!

Thanksgiving break 2014 I was hired at Sunny Blue, as a cashier. I knew nothing about the restaurant nor had I even heard about it until I found it on Snagajob. I was relieved and happy to be employed. All I could think about was being able to buy my first car on my own and that my mom would stop complaining about giving me money.

A month into the job my manager asked me if I wanted to learn how to make omusubi. "Yeah, why not give it a shot?" At first I found it difficult to measure the rice and how much exactly to put in my hand, plus the rice was burning hot, so I'd end up dropping most of it on the counter. My rice balls ended up being either way too big or elf-sized. I wanted to give up.

My manager saw I was struggling and sent me back to the register to give my hands some rest from the heat; I went back to the register disappointed. D a y s later I asked to try again, hoping to get used to the burning sensation of hot rice. He denied my offer, but later I asked again and he agreed.

This time while making omusubi, I tried to ignore the burning sensations. I felt I was under pressure to complete not only one but twenty-six decent-looking omusubis. I started scooping rice and then filled them all according to what was ordered, but after all the orders were completed, I couldn't stop. I was on a roll, making enough omusubi to fill the entire warming drawer. I seasoned them and neatly arranged them to fit in the drawer.

My manager came back and jokingly said, "You gave up already?"

"Look in the drawer," I said.

He checked and looked shocked. "Brittany, you did all these? The drawer is full!"

"Well, yes," I said. "Aren't you proud?"

"You went from no to pro like overnight, what the heck! I don't think we need you at the register anymore."

I was shocked. I had been hired as a cashier and was promoted to food prep.

My family has been in the restaurant business since I was young, and it felt amazing to be back in this environment.

I am grateful to be employed and grateful to Keiko for hiring me and being an employer who offers minors the work experience most places require we already have for a first job.

Portrait of Brittany Weight © Hannah Schatzle

Don't Know

by Miguel Gianfranco Guzman Valle

Sometimes I feel that life is like a straight line
And I don't know if I am still alive
But I always fight to survive
So I will be able to say that I am fine.

I convince myself that people are kind
And I think that we are all alike
But in the end they always strike
And now I see that I have been always blind.

Not all are so mean
There are people who I can trust
Around them I don't feel just
Those are the kind of people on whom I can lean.

I know that I am not alone
And that I have people on whom I can count
And from them I will learn
That not all my friends are gone.

The Perks of Discovering Literature

by Anthony Cortez

I come from a broken home with shattered dreams. My father is a violent, belligerent drunk, never at home. My mother works to keep my siblings and me clothed and fed. Although I've always had a family, I've always felt alone and on my own.

As years passed I grew more and more neglected. I feel as if I am a floating piece of paper drifting through the world. I escape within books, and when I do my anxiety and depression fade. With book in hand I feel strong, engulfed with power and ambition. When I finish reading I close the cover and say good-bye as if it were an old friend. At the end of the read I am not the same person who began the journey 200 or 300 pages earlier.

I was walking down a dark road in the middle of the night, as I often do to clear my mind, when I literally stumbled upon a book that changed me forever, *The Perks of Being a Wallflower,* by Stephen Chbosky. It is a remarkable tale of a young, socially awkward, quiet teen struggling with depression. I was captivated from the beginning. Chbosky's emotional depth and honest tone resonated with me. Over time, I, like Charlie, the main character, learned that patience, effort, and friends can help one grow, help one escape one's personal darkness and move into a better light. I learned that it's not about where one comes from but where one's headed that counts.

As I read I gradually felt myself changing as Charlie changed. At first I felt numb, cold, isolated, engulfed in sorrow, some of my own making, some thrust upon me. However, I chose to accept my past tragedies and move on. I learned, as Charlie did, that life is way too brief to hold onto mistakes and family trauma and wallow in them. Every minute I spent berating myself was a wasted minute. What *The Perks of Being a Wallflower* taught me is that change is constantly in motion. And positive change is always an option.

Oddly, I found an interest in literature walking down a lonely path heading nowhere in particular. Now I find that literature has molded me into the positive, intellectually curious young man I am today.

Literature is forever in my soul.

A Dream Comes a Long Way

by Anthony Rios

I think of myself as a dreamer.

It started when I was in fifth grade.

I had no one to lean on. Every day I was picked on because I was fat. Kids called me Jelly Roll Toe, Fatty, and etc. I wore the same clothes for weeks because I didn't have a lot. I was roaming the street with my friends, hopeless, with no one to turn to.

But every night I dreamed that I would become somebody.

Every day was a battle, because I didn't know where I was headed.

I lay in bed and dreamed of a better life. I always questioned myself.

"Is this life really for me?"

"Is there another way out of the 'hood?"

I dreamed of having a father who would teach me how to grow as a man; how to shave; how to write and how to earn respect.

I woke.

It was all a dream. I knew it wasn't true. I wish it was true.

Now I know only I can carve out my own future. I need to stay on the straight and narrow road. Even though I may stumble and fall occasionally.

It is not in my blood to give up. All my dreams will come true if I do something about them. I will learn to become a man on my own.

All those years I felt empty, like something was missing.

But I found writing.

Writing's helped keep me on track. Writing's helped me understand that my past can't hurt me anymore.

A dream made me come a long way from my past to this present moment.

What We Eat

I Am a Fat Girl

by Qahirah Smith

I am a fat girl at heart
I wonder if bacon and tuna taste good together
I hear the sound of bacon grease popping out of a pan
I see my junk food stashed in my drawer
I want cornbread with syrup.

I am a fat girl at heart
I pretend I don't eat much but I pig out on every piece of junk
    food in sight
I touch the croissants with chocolate inside at POPS. and
    thank the person who invented such a thing.

I worry I might die of diabetes since I love sweets
I won't eat applesauce—just nasty
I cry when I see lite syrup at the store; I need all my sugar.

I am a fat girl at heart
I understand what I eat isn't good for me
I say I will eat healthy but never do
I dream of Bacon Alfredo; it's like
Chicken Alfredo but the bacon replaces the chicken.

I try to cut down on fried chicken with Red Rooster hot sauce
I hope someday there is an unlimited supply of bacon
I am a fat girl at heart.

Oysters

by Marianne Valencia

Seafood is my favorite food.
I love shrimp, lobster, oysters, clams, and crabs.
Squeezing lemon and adding a pinch of salt on top of shrimp is the best taste
   imaginable
The pepper and butter melt into my taste buds.
   My dad and I always had seafood twice a week.
   A seafood truck on Gage Avenue and Avalon was our spot, and a restaurant
called Mi Lindo Nayarit, those were our all-time favorites.
   My dad and I shared the same likes in food.
   We would always order the same items.
   I would get a tostada of shrimp ceviche and three *empanadas de camaron.*
   My dad would order a shrimp and crab cocktail, very hot!
   We would share a dozen oysters.
   Oysters were our connection.
   Scraping the oyster off the shell,
   Squeezing lemon, salt, and Tapatio. Quickly eating them.
   They were the best thing.
   I loved the texture.
   I've eaten oysters as far back as I can remember.
   Now that I'm older and I don't see my dad, my taste for oysters has gone away.
   I no longer crave them because my dad did.
   He introduced me to them.
   Now, I don't care about them. Seafood, along with other foods, well, I've lost
interest in them.

Pupusas

by Nelvia Marin

My great-grandmother made homemade pupusas
Every other weekend my grandmother would come over and cook traditional
Salvadorian dishes
My favorite, pupusas—like Italian calzone with a different stuffing.
She made the curtido the night before
The curtido is coleslaw, but instead of mayo it has vinegar with oregano.
The ingredients are cabbages, carrots, jalapenos, cucumbers, onions, oregano,
vinegar, and salt
Cut very thin.
You can't forget the salsa—fresh tomatoes, jalapeno, onions, and green bell
peppers put into a pot to boil
Quickly blended
You have your salsa for your pupusas.
My grandmother would get a big plastic bowl
Add the maza and water, mix it together and start making the pupusas.
She would make a flat tortilla using a cloth
Adding the toppings—cheese, beans, and chicharron
My favorite chicharron with cheese
Placing them into the comal, a flat pan, to cook.
She served the pupusas so hot
My white plastic plate had a circle imprint on it.
My mother stood next to her to see how everything was made
But it didn't help her much.
Mother follows every single step that grandma did
But without as much love as Grandma gave her pupusas.
Chicharron and cheese pupusas are not the same anymore.

I Am Vegan

by Zaria Lampkins

I am VEGAN
I wonder why/how can people eat a dead body (meat)
I hear people ask me the same question: "Where do you get your
  protein?"
I see videos on the internet about animal cruelty
I want animal cruelty to stop

I am VEGAN
I pretend I care about negative comments people have to say
  about me being vegan
I feel happy with the lifestyle I have chosen
I touch nothing that has been killed with a face on it
I worry that one day all animals will die because of humans
I cry when I see videos of animals being slaughtered (I'm lying I
  don't cry)

I am VEGAN
I understand that the life of an animal is as important as ours
I say save a life and go vegan
I dream that one day everyone will be vegan
I try to help people understand why they should go vegan
I hope that someday I can convince more people to go vegan

I am VEGAN

I've Ate Everywhere*

by Andrew Hernandez

*To the tune of *I've Been Everywhere*, written by Geoff Mack in 1959, adapted by Hank Snow, made most famous by Johnny Cash.

I was chillin' like a villain; wondering what to eat,
Wantin' something new, not the same ol' Arby's meat,
I had some places in mind, but I ate there already,
So I looked at my home dawg and asked, "What do I do, Freddy?"
I just want to eat somewhere new, with good food, I swear,
Then I thought to myself, "I've ate everywhere."

I've ate everywhere, dawg,
I've ate everywhere, dawg,
Even though I'm not a millionaire, dawg,
I've took home so much Tupperware, dawg,
All across LA, I've been there, dawg,
I've ate everywhere.

I've ate in Venice, Westchester, Malibu, Marina del Rey,
Santa Monica, Hawthorne, Torrance and Downtown LA,
Beverly Hills, Pasadena, Playa Vista, Inglewood,
Long Beach, Culver City, San Francisco, West Hollywood

I've ate everywhere, dawg,
I've ate everywhere, dawg,
Even though I'm not a millionaire, dawg,
I've took home so much Tupperware, dawg,
All across LA, I've been there, dawg,
I've ate everywhere.

I've ate at California Chicken Café, Café 50's, Abajenos,
Casa Sanchez, Hoagies, Tony P's, and Costco,
The Pantry, Truxton's Alejos, Pacos Tacos, Chicago Ribs,
Johnny Rockets, Hooters, iHop, Olive Garden, Buggy Whip.

I've ate everywhere, dawg.
I've ate everywhere

Life at POPS

Not Alone

by Marianne Valencia

Attending POPS has made me realize I was hiding behind my own body. I came to POPS not knowing what the club was about. I knew a few people who went to the club. I decided to go one day. During the third week in the club I got comfortable with my fellow classmates and other students who attended.

During class Mr. Danziger was having us write our personal essays for college and I was having trouble putting my story on paper. He told me, "Go somewhere in your house that is quiet and for six minutes write whatever you remember about that experience," so I did that and I produced a wonderful story.

This story made me brush off pain I had held onto for years. This pain was covering me up, not letting me be myself. It was like dusting a self off that had been covered in dust and you could not see its beauty behind the mounds of dust.

I found myself quite light after I wrote it. It relieved me.

POPS was a space I could be free and share my story with students going through the same pain of incarceration of the mind, of not letting your thoughts or feelings be heard by someone.

I found out that I needed help and moral support from others. I thought I was alone, but I was wrong!

My Life Starts on 2K15

by Kat Secaida

Let me go back a few years to 2K12
I was happy, but not all the time.
I felt my aggressiveness getting stronger at the age of 12

I was always told never throw the first punch.
Now it's 2K13

Boom! Fight
Cuff cuff
Boom! 13 in a cop car
Click click mug shots
Stamp stamp fingerprints taken
The f__ did I get myself into?
Waited two months, didn't know what was going to happen to me
Dumbass is what the angel on my right is saying
You got that, b____, is what the devil on the left tells me

Shhhh …

It's now 2K14, I'm a freshman, still 13
You dumb youngster! What are you doing getting smoked out, ditching class?

In the beginning of the year something hit me …

Went home, wasn't proud of myself as tears streamed down my face.

NO, I don't want to smoke with you
NO, I don't want your number
NO, I don't want to ditch with you
NO, I don't want to get my jeans caught on the fence anymore

It's now 2K15
I've changed
But now Father's in jail for the second time
Now he's in the hospital
What's next?
I've been scared if he ever goes back to his addiction
My mother who never left my sight, even when I did wrong
My mentor Dana who I've known since I was six years old
I've met Mariana, my best friend, who sees the good in me and not all the bad
She sees that I do have a heart

POPS the Club where I can be myself and not fear anything
"Write, you'll feel better!"
My life has changed. I was never into writing and showing people how I feel
And what's going on
But I learned you can relate to a lot of teenagers
I wish I had come here last year!

Such a friendly place to be
No judgment
It's just an amazing vibe

I thank Amy, Mr. Danziger, and Stacey
For all the support and not feeling alone,
Thank you.

My Time in POPS

by Miguel Gianfranco Guzman Valle

I came to high school from El Salvador and had never seen a group like this.
A group that shared with others about their past
A place where people reminisce
And see how the time flies fast.

The value of what people say
And the experiences that people share
Have emotions that weigh every day
And sometimes they are just hard to declare.

Feelings and experiences are compared
And I appreciate and learn
I see that everything can be repaired
And I admire it, as if it were a gem.

Different lives and different experiences
I listen to them and try to learn a bit of everything
In a way to fill out my own inexperience
When I haven't even shared anything.

My life is not tragic.
I have had everything I need
Even if sometimes it seems to be magic,
Sometimes I feel that I can't proceed.

POPS the Club has shown me that people fight to keep progressing
They don't give up and they do their best
And it seems that everything they say comes with a blessing
And makes people feel like they can succeed.

Thinking on how much they got hurt
And for others how much joy they received
Now I see that they are alert
And see how much they have achieved.

Not everything they share has been sad
There are stories filled with life and joy
Things that people feel glad
And they are able to enjoy.

Groups like this make me feel
The joy of life, love, and fear
Knowing that everything is real
And that all these things can pass in just a year.

I learned from POPS that life is not always kind
And sometimes I will have to fight for what life has taught and not to lose it
I have to be conscious of what is in my mind
And learn from life, bit by bit.

POPS Special Significance to a Student

by Melissa Nava/Entertainment Editor

(originally published in *The Oarsman*,
Venice High newspaper, March 13, 2015)

Our school has an amazing club called Pain of the Prison System, also known as POPS. This club means a lot to me because I feel like I am a totally new person, with a whole lot of weight that has been lifted off my chest. Since I joined POPS, I feel relief.

On March 1, some members from the club, including me, went to read their personal essay to people they didn't even know at Beyond Baroque on Venice Boulevard. This was an amazing experience because I have never talked about my personal life problems nor have I been able to express my feelings to my mother nor my father. When I speak to both of them, I hide all my pain behind a smile.

Reading my story out loud made me realize that I should always express myself, no matter how hard the situation. Never keep things inside of you that can harm you mentally and physically, because there are people out there you can reach out to, who can guide you along the right path.

Thanks to POPS sponsor Mr. Danziger and his wife, I was able to share with the world how painful my life has been with an absent father and how I feel about everything and how I go on day by day with that gut feeling that I will never see my father again. He left after I turned 4 and never came back. He got caught twice trying to come into the country illegally and spent several years in jail, and now lives in Zacatecas, Mexico.

I know that there are a lot of teenagers who also suffer from the absence of a parent and end up doing drugs or joining a gang. Instead of all that, you should come and join POPS. We all support each other and are there for each other through our ups and downs.

This is a very supportive club, and you can express yourself freely without having people judge you. I bet there are other teenagers who share the same story as you. POPS meets every Wednesday at lunch in Room 120.

Life in Reverse

Flowers in Reverse © Victor L.M. Demic

The following poems were inspired by the poem *21*, by Patrick Roche.

Countdown from 17

by Angelee Velasquez

17 years old. I can't stand being with my father for even 10 minutes without arguing. We're the opposite. I'm getting older and wiser and he thinks I'm the same age as when he first left me. I've grown used to not having him help out.

16 years old. My dad is trying harder to be a father and to be there more. I let him do his fatherly duties without trying to complain so I don't give him a hard time, but it's not the same when I'm used to him always being there only when it's convenient for him and not when I need him the most.

15 years old. I came to the conclusion that my dad sold and did cocaine when I was younger—they called it "cake," and now I get what that means.

14 years old. I started doing better in school and changing my ways.

13 years old. My freshman year of high school was a mess. I ditched, smoked, and drank alcohol.

12 years old. My dad did some time in jail for a DUI, child endangerment, and a stolen vehicle.

11 years old. I didn't see my dad for two years. After this I didn't really care because I started growing closer to my mom.

10 years old. My dad never came to my elementary school graduation. Did he forget? Or was it not that important to him?

9 years old. I saw my dad get arrested. He was charged with a DUI and a stolen vehicle. This was considered child endangerment. I remember waking up to a flashlight in my face. I looked and my dad wasn't in the driver's seat. I turned around and saw him being handcuffed. "What's your name? Do you know another family member's phone number? How old are you? Do you know your address?" was all I heard from the police officer who was standing at my window.

8 years old. My mom left my dad and put him on child support because he stopped giving her money. My dad thought my mom was using the money for herself and not spending it on what I needed.

7 years old. I went to another party. This time I was locked in a room with a bunch of kids watching *Spongebob*. We weren't allowed to come out of the room. I climbed out the window anyway while the other kids were asleep.

6 years old. My father called my mom and told her that he wanted nothing to do with me and never wanted to see me again.

5 years old. I went to my first gang-affiliated party with my dad since his mom never wanted to babysit me. Bringing me along was his only choice.

4 years old. I always saw my dad carry out white bags of powder from his safe into the bathroom, and when I asked him what it was, he said it was cake.

3 years old. My parents were always arguing. I remember watching the *Fifth Element*, sitting in my booster seat on the floor, when my father put his hands on my mother, and there was nothing I could do but watch.

2 years old.

1 year old.

0

Shattered

by Anthony Cortez

Counting down from age 17…

17. My heart is shattered by my girlfriend. I never imagined she would leave me.

16. My other half, Lillie, my sister, moves away. I lose my voice. The moon, my only friend, goes away too.

15. My Uncle Danny passes away. I wonder how many people will attend my funeral.

14. For the first time in three years, I see my absent father. In a courtroom.

13. I get drunk and wonder if my father and I would get along.

12. My best friend and I split paths. I feel as if I have lost a brother.

11. My grandfather Tony passes away. I do not cry.

10. I get into a fight. I enjoy the pain.

9. I am greeted by a stranger. Actually, he is my father.

8. I cry for a man I have never met.

7. My father, a drug addict, buys drugs rather than visit his own son on his birthday.

6. I am ashamed to draw my first memory, so I draw fictional ones because I do not want to draw my father beating my mother.

5. I move to Venice, California. My father and family disappear.

4. I scratch at my father's eyes as he tries to run over my mother.

3. I am sitting on my grandmother's rocking chair, tears streaming down my cheeks; whimpering fills the quiet house as I call out for my mother.

Nothing

by Elia Guadalupe Espinosa

At the age of 17 I was diagnosed with Alpha I Anti-trypsin, also known as liver disease. My mom said it was nothing.

At the age of 16, nothing led me to a state of depression and anxiety. I found myself stranded behind thick bars and two-feet wide windows that wouldn't allow air in or out. Cerritos Mental Hospital, where you left what you couldn't handle or understand. It was a week of hell.

At the age of 15 my family was breaking apart, from cheating on her husband to being abused. It seemed so easy to want to help, but my mom said, "You know nothing!"

At the age of 14 and 13 I had on and off conversations with the man who left me at birth. I knew he had a family, but what was I?

At the age of 12 and 11 I would beg and beg my mother to tell me who he was. The man everyone never talked about. What did he do bad enough for his name never to be mentioned?

At the age of 10 was my second attempt at suicide. I would pick pills that would be sure never to wake me up. It never worked. I would hear my aunt scream, "You belong in hell!" That's what they called a fetus of an affair.

At the age of 9 I was a lost soul. I moved for the second time. I left everything behind, but my mom never cared. She was happy with that one guy.

At the age of 8 my mom had her fourth boyfriend, I mean they lasted, and I was happy for her. My first attempt at overdosing, my body filled with untold bruises. Bruises she didn't know about.

At the age of 7 and 6 I moved from aunt to aunt as my mother was always so busy looking for jobs, with her boyfriends.

At the age of 5 I moved to Los Angeles, California, from Mexico D.F., my birth state. It was an easy move, the people so friendly and generous. It wasn't as clean as my mother had said it was.

At 4 and 3 Grandma CeCe looked after me. She took me to my first day of kindergarten. CeCe taught me how to cook, clean, and be me. She bought me my own mini sink so by her side I could scrub my own clothes.

At 2 my father was painted out of the picture. Mother never mentioned him. Why? I don't know why.

At 0 I was born by the will of a 28-year-old woman who knew not one thing of motherhood but the first thing she did was leave. I guess I was never anything to her.

Obstacles

by Grecia Jara

17 - Graduating high school and enrolling in college, knowing my dad's proud, but feeling that hole in my heart knowing he's not here to see the accomplishments I have achieved and witness my diploma being received. Just got word from my uncle he is going to jail again—he's been on the run for a year now. "Money was too good," he said. Won't be able to attend my graduation. Might be locked up for 16 years. Said my good-bye last night.

16 - Getting mad going to church every Sunday. I believe in God but then I don't. I'm confused. I'm really mad at him for not answering my prayers. Uncle Andy got stabbed by a gang, told me it wasn't over drugs, but I don't believe that.

15 – Uncle Andy came back. Promises me he won't leave again. On principal's Honor Roll and got baptized. Mom's happy. Stopped sleeping with my mom, started sleeping in my own room. Having communication issues with my mom. We don't talk to each other much about personal things.

14 – I got a boyfriend. I don't know how boyfriends are supposed to be. I wish my dad was here to tell me. Messing up in school. I know my mom isn't proud but don't feel like trying anymore. I wish this was a bad dream.

13 – Mom tells me she wants me to get baptized at our new church. I don't want to. God didn't help me and I'm mad at him. I don't pray to him anymore.

12, 11 – I wake up in the middle of the night because Mom won't stop crying. She cries every night. She says it's my grades, but I know it's not that. I want to go to heaven. I think committing suicide will help.

10 – I'm starting middle school. Dad wasn't there for my graduation for elementary. My mom says he was, but I didn't see him. Mom stopped going to church. Dad's side of the family doesn't want to visit me anymore. Reminds them too much of my dad. I feel abandoned. They don't love me anymore.

9 - Dad passed away, I don't know where he went. People tell me he went to heaven. I want to go to heaven to see him. People from our church told us we didn't have enough faith in God and that's why he died. My mom got really mad and started crying on our way home after church. What did they mean?

8 - My Mom told me I've missed too much school and I have to start going every day. I don't want to leave my dad. I like seeing him every day. I heard him telling my mom he wasn't going to make it. I've prayed to God for 3 years now, he hasn't gotten better.

7 - Daddy goes to Cedars Sinai Hospital every week now. I don't like going there, it's too cold and their food isn't as good as Titos Tacos or Pollo Loco where my dad used to take me every week. They don't like giving me bagels with cream cheese every hour in his room, they told me they have to work. But I get hungry, and I like bagels with cream cheese better than the Jell-O and juice boxes they give my dad every day.

6 – Daddy's really sick, his hair and fingernails are gone, and he looks like a skeleton. I can't sleep with him anymore because I move a lot and hurt his leg at night so I have to sleep with Mommy only. Daddy sleeps in my room now by himself. I miss sleeping with him. I hear him throw up a lot. My mom told me dad has Cancer, and I think that's a stomach flu. Grandma told me to pray to God and he will get better. The nurse lady at school keeps giving me canned foods and Barbies to take home. She's so nice, I think she likes me better than the other kids.

5 - Daddy has a bump on his leg. He told me not to tell Mommy. He doesn't want to worry her.

4 - Grandpa just died, where did he go? I miss him and the cookies he'd buy me. Daddy takes me to eat Pollo Loco and play at the park to forget about it.

3 - Uncle Andy doesn't visit me anymore. Grandma and I used to visit him at Ralph's where he worked, but he doesn't go there anymore. They told me he went to jail. What's jail? Daddy tells me not to worry, and I'll see him soon.

2, 1 - I like being with my mom and dad. I also like the Barbie song and the Little Mermaid.

I Don't Need Him

by Nelvia Marin

18: Holding anger at a man who couldn't stay around to be a dad, but a dad to another non-marriage family. One word, COWARD

17: Jealousy. Seeing everything on social network. It seems so perfect, trying to kill my vibe, but in my head I'm like wait for it, KARMA

16: Papa is on his fourth kid, a boy

15: Feeling unwanted by Papa, didn't show up for my 15th birthday but attended uncle's wedding, LIAR

14: Finding out Papa has a new family, tears running down my face, thinking, "Why couldn't this woman respect my parent's marriage?"

13: New man in the house but I can't call him Papa, it doesn't feel right

12: Feeling lost, new school, no family. Just waiting for that monthly money because the mall makes me feel at home

11: Mama cries herself to sleep. Can't do much to change that. Just hold her. I'm only eleven

10: Just Mama and me in Las Vegas. Where's Papa and sister so we can be a complete family?

9: Moving to Las Vegas, Nevada, new home

8: Mama tries to explain what's happening but all I want is to eat this cake batter ice cream with brownies in peace

7: Moving in with Grandma, parents are fighting for custody

6: Pap comes back home just to mess up again

5: Papa leaves without an excuse

4: Mama and Papa have a strong argument

3 & 2: Mama says to me, "Everything is going to be all right. Your health is going to get better little by little. These words are on replay for two years

1: I'm carried around because I can't do much for myself

0: Hoping for a baby boy

Clash of the Titans

by De'Jon K. Jones

18   Your youngest child. Your only boy. Your baby. Our bond is now stronger than ever. I wouldn't trade you for the world. You're my mom, my creator. You made me.

17   Kicked out for the second time in the cold. Wandered the streets of Inglewood alone. Fearless 'cause I had a gun and I thought I'd make it on my own.

16   Snatched out of the house by the police at 4 a.m., wearing just some boxers and a tee. They separated you from me. Your panicky, concerned voice became distant. Thinking to myself that I'd become another black statistic. Murdered by the police. With all the assault rifles and beams aimed at my back as I stood face to wall.

16   We're like Clash of the Titans verbally with the words we're exchanging. Or maybe you were Zeus, 'cause I was always Hades. Kicked out for the first time. I know I hurt your feelings 'cause you hurt mine. As we argued, and I told you, "I didn't ask to be here. You should've gotten an abortion and this burden would be unheard."

16   Worried for me after I got jumped by some enemies. Knowing my attitude is f___ed. You knew I'd call my brothers and some ShoLines and go out on a manhunt.

15   Two of my Zoo members went to juvenile hall for being caught with firearms. You asked me if I had one. Lied and said no. You searched my room anyway and found nothing. It was tucked away in the wash house.

14   You liked to talk about my nostrils and how they'd flare up when I got upset. Just like yours. I'm your son and we've got the same flat nose.

13   I never banged. At school it was just Black vs. Mexican. Better yet, ShoLine vs. Trece. I didn't get it. Both sets were from Venice. You prayed every morning, hoping it'd end. But I was too deep in it.

12   Stuck at home. More like confinement or prison. Wouldn't leave my room 'cause it was me, you, and my three sisters. Y'all did hair, nails, gossiped, and had periods. Prisoner in my own home. Wanted nothing to do with it.

11   Told me ever since you and my dad split and he moved out, I went angry. That I was trying to grow up too fast. That I should enjoy being a kid, while childhood lasts.

10   We got evicted. My siblings and I slept in a crowded space at Grandmother's house. You slept in your car. I thought it was my fault and didn't get it. You had to work harder and make sacrifices to make a living.

9   You and my dad taught me how to ride a bike. You woke up a few days later heartbroken, and didn't know how to tell me. My bike was stolen.

8   You would buy me all the wrestler action figures. I still have all of them. In a green crate stored in my closet. They're useless to me, but my nephew plays with them.

7   You knew I was a daredevil. Told me not to jump off my bunk bed but I did anyway. Knocked one tooth out and the front two turned brown. Good thing I was young, and they fell out.

6   Made me grow my hair back out. I hated it. I was mistaken for a "pretty little girl" every time we stepped out.

5   I hated getting my hair braided. I was tender-headed. I told Keyona to cut my hair, and she did.

4   You always remind me about the time when I jumped over our balcony to play when I wasn't supposed to. Our neighbor Beverly brought me back home. The next day you two were laughing at me because she said hi. I ignored her until you told me to speak. Instead I said, "She talks too much." You two laughed even harder and called me crazy.

3   I loved LegoLand. No idea how, but I vividly remember the time we went. I loved the little roller coasters, the Lego people, and the playpen.

2   Just a happy, carefree, chunky redheaded baby. Always had new Jordans on. Sixteen years later and now I'm addicted.

1   You couldn't get enough of me. You never got an ultrasound to determine the sex of any of your babies.

0   After 9 long months of pregnancy, I was born. On March 22, 1997, you finally got your son. I was the greatest gift and surprise as you thought you would be having another baby girl.

Brotherhood

by Anthony Rios

17. My brother left for San Diego. I was all alone again, but I always know any minute or hour, when I'm feeling in pain, my brother finds a way to come see me!

16. I was trying to do well in school because I didn't want to fuck up, my brother always listens to me!

15. I was ditching school because school wasn't for me. I was hanging out with the homies up to nothing good, but my brother found me and took me home!

14. Starting high school was all new to me, plus I found all the ways to get in trouble. I didn't give a sh__ but my brother gave me advice saying, "You're better than that."

13.

12.

11.

10. The move from Lennox to Inglewood, it wasn't easy because I had all my friends in Lennox and now I was going to a new school. My brother took me because my dad wasn't around and my mother wasn't either.

9. When my foster dad was beating up on my foster mom, I ran up to him and pushed him away. My brother came and took me outside because my brother was about to kick his butt!

8. I was shooting hoops outside in the driveway. My brother came outside to play with me because I was always alone. I had a deep, cold heart but my brother always made everything all right!

7. When they took me away from my mom, they put me in foster care, but they took four of us in the same home. Lucky I had my "brothers and sisters." I was sad because I was all alone, but my brother, Angel, just told me, "Never lose hope. One day everything will be all right!"

6. I was getting picked on because I was obese. I cried. I did something about it. My brother worked out with me and said, "A quitter won't get anything in life but if you really want it, never let up!"

5. When I was on the streets, getting beat up because they pushed my sister, and she was crying, my brother came and they ran away!

4. When I was getting picked on at school, my brother told them to lay off. My brother was like a father for me!

3. I remember that I was afraid of the dark, but my brother was right beside me, fighting my demons on the spot!

2. My brother took care of me when my mom was at work.

I was born. All I can see is my mom and brother because my father wasn't around.

I'm thankful for my brother taking the place of my father! I know it's not easy to fill those shoes!

Our History

by Dannie Maddox

17. My dad is back with his other family, but it's okay.

16. My dad came home HOME and we connected like he never left.

15. I went to prom and my dad wasn't there to tell me I am BEAUTIFUL.

14. My dad went back to jail, but this time I witnessed him getting arrested.

13. I was a jealous little brat because I didn't feel like Daddy's little princess anymore, thanks to Tiana.

12. I hated my dad.

11. My dad left me and my mom, AGAIN, but this time it wasn't for a jail cell. It was for a different family.

10. I finally got to see my dad for my fifth-grade graduation.

9. My dad explained why he was in jail for a long period of time.

8. I finally asked my mom why my dad went on vacation without us. She told me the real reason. "Baby, because Daddy is in jail."

7. I started receiving letters from my dad because he "lost his phone."

6. I finally talked to my dad (even though it was for a short period of time).

5. I started school without my dad.

4. My mom was lying to me, saying that my dad was on "vacation."

3. My dad went missing.

2. I always went on "business trips" with my dad—because that's what he called them.

1. Dannie Girl was my daddy's little princess!

0. An angel was brought into the Maddox family.

Forever My All

by Veronica Vargas

18, I listen to her wish for the ending to her life, I hear tears hidden during showers, and I think to myself that hopefully one day I can help erase the pain.

17, she feels alone and unloved, so I write her letters, one for each emotion she could feel.

16, I lose my grandma to heart failure. I fall into depression and all is gray. Then I see her, I see color again.

15, my family turns their backs on me. In return she gives me more love and support than all of them combined.

14, I made a huge mistake and disappointed her. I feel shamed and full of regret, still do 'til this day. But she forgave me and the image she had of me didn't change.

13, I graduate middle school and start high school. She was so worried. The thing is so was I, but for her. I wanted so much for her that she didn't think was possible.

12, she gets mad at me for straightening my hair every day, for throwing clothes everywhere and not putting my shoes away. And she says it's her fault I'm this way. She told me when I was younger not to worry so much about everything being so straight.

11, I want to wear eyeliner now. She says I'm too young. She talks to Dad. Outcome being that I won.

10, we have mother-daughter days. I miss those. Went out for lunch, shopping. Or stayed in eating chips and her always drinking Diet Coke watching *House* until the sun went down.

9, I wanted to be just like her, I still do. She looked like a queen, like the ones in all the Disney movies.

8, we go to the park. She lies down and reads, and that's when I look at her and realize she isn't just a mom to me and my little brother, Gerardo, but to all my little cousins Saul, Diego, Jessie, and Richie.

7, she tells cheesy puns like, "oh I see, says the blind man ..." I try to explain things.

6

5, I want to become a fairy because she loves them so much, little do I notice she adored me way more.

4

3, I start preschool. I didn't want her to leave. She did anyway and came back a while later and I told her I already had friends, that I'll see her when the bell rings. She laughs at this.

2

1

0, she asks God to give her someone so she can feel loved for the first time in her life, someone who will remain by her side. March 19, 1997, a little girl is born. And she says she finds her reason to stay alive.

He's Never Coming Back

by Melissa Nava

19
Getting Older.
Worrying about graduation.
Will my dad be here to see me walk the stage?
Nah!

18
I'm a legal adult.
Going to La Mirage Night Club for the first time.
Still living at home, though.
Dad still doesn't call to see how we are.

17
Mom is diagnosed with kidney failure.
Do I need this to happen to me right now?
No.
My mom is my pride and joy. The reason I wake up every morning.
Dad doesn't seem to budge to come back.

16
I feel like shit.
Dad calls for money.
What the heck is going through his head?
My mother barely has money to support us.
Should we send him money?
Nah, he can work for himself and his new family.
We no longer matter to him.

15
My *quinceanera*, July 16, 2011
The day I looked forward to.
Danced all night long.
Felt like a paparazzi, pictures here and there.
The first time I got drunk because of my uncle.
Was my dad there?
No.
Did he call to say happy birthday?
No.
Family from Mexico said he got drunk that day because he wasn't here to
    celebrate with me.

Did I care?
No.

14
Graduated from Mark Twain Middle School.
Started high school.
It was scary.
Dad wasn't around to help me with boy problems when I needed him.
Started to hate my family because it was broken apart.

13
Realized Dad wasn't coming back.
Found out my dad had other children.
Hated all girls who had a dad.
Wished every night and day that my dad could be here.
Got kicked out of class every day during 5th period because I'd argue
    with Mr. Mazilli.
Spit in his face, talked back, threw objects at him.
I was considered the dean's best friend.
The lazy no good.

12
Graduated from Broadway Elementary School.
Got a friendship scholarship.
Lost communication with my so-called besties.
Started middle school.
Met new friends; still friends with them today.
I was a straight A student.
Didn't hear from the man I was supposed to call Dad.

11
Got my period.
Pads so uncomfortable.
Walking like I got a stick up my butt.
Dad wasn't there to comfort me when I had cramps.
Chest started to hurt because my boobs started to grow.

10
Moved houses.
From the 'hood to Culver City.
Lost my so-called best friends forever but later gained some.
Became a troublemaker.
Looked forward to every weekend because Dad always called and said,
    "*Mija, te quiero mucho y te extraño.*" (Baby, I love you and I miss you.)

9
Made my first Communion.
Dad wasn't there, although he promised me.

8
Grandmita Sarah died.
Tears rushed down my face.
Grandmita was my world.
She was the best.

7
Met the best teacher, Mr. Jefferson.
Saw friends walking with their dads to school.
I always wondered if one day my dad would bring me to school.

6
Dad wasn't coming back.
I miss him.

5
Dad was arrested by immigration border protection because he got
    caught trying to come to the U.S. illegally.
He served 26 months.
Later deported to Zacatecas, Mexico.

4
I wanted to be the Little Mermaid.
Dad left after my birthday.

3
I was Daddy's little princess.
He promised never to leave my side.
I'd cuddle with him every night with my LALA Teletubby.
We would go fishing together.
I'd always look through ice in the ocean and all of a sudden a fish would
    pop up.
I thought I made magic.

2
I was Daddy's little Barbie who he played dress-up with.

1
Baptized in Zacatecas, Mexico.
Learned how to walk by grabbing my dog, Monoifacias's, tail.
Dad was always there to catch me when I fell.

0

Mom realized she was two months pregnant with me.
Dad promised never to leave her side.
He would satisfy her craving.
He'd sing lullabies to her stomach till he fell asleep on her belly.
I'd kick him and he would wake up.

17 years

by Qahirah Smith

17 Years
Mom is pregnant with her 5th child
Got in a big argument because her priorities aren't straight
I wish I didn't have to teach her how to be a mom
I feel sorry for her
I don't care about her trying to be in my life anymore, I just want her to be a good
    mother to my two little sisters and for the one that's on its way

16 years
Mom got a new boyfriend and had her 4th child by him
Told her to get her tubes tied
Got in a fight with her because all she cares about is spending time with her
    boyfriend and not her kids, especially me since I rarely come down to see her

15 years
She told me the reason she isn't in my life is because my dad is doing a better job;
    I felt that was a stupid excuse because she is my mom and she is responsible for
    me until I turn18.
She kicked my brother out because he was standing up for his sisters on how my
    mom constantly keeps abandoning us for her boy toys, and she doesn't like to
    listen to the truth

14 years
I would only go down to my mom's to see my brother, sister, nephew, uncle, and
    cousins

13 years
Move to California
I moved out to Cali. With every intention of not seeing my mother
My stepmom forced me to see her so I could fix our situation so I won't have the
    same problem with my kids

12 years
Gave up trying with my mom
I stopped calling her *Mom*; she was just the lady who gave birth to me
She disowned me so I disown her as a mother

11 years
Got my period
Wished I had a mom who was there to help me, thank God for the internet, I
    guess

10 years

She came out to see me in New Jersey; well, I thought she was

I found out she was only coming out to see my father; and she was only acting like she cared so my dad wouldn't know

Hated women after my mom did that to me; women are snakes in the grass; they'll do whatever to get what they want

9 years

All my friends have both parents in their lives

I wonder how it would feel to have the love and care from my mother and father. I know relationships don't last because both partners don't agree on anything, but why when the partners split up must the parent disappear from her child's life, too?

Does my mom care to know where I'm at?

I wonder how my brother is doing.

Does my sister remember me?

8 years

Started wearing bras

Wish I had a mom to come with me to shop for bras and not my father; I know my father feels awkward, but I do appreciate him being there for me.

7 years

Moved to New Jersey

My sister Ericka was born; apparently she changed my mom's life for good.

6 years

Visit my mom on summer vacation

My mom's boyfriend burns me on my back because I won't call him *Daddy*

My mom is living from hotel to hotel

My brother lives with my grandma and grandpa

Not once has my mom thought maybe she shouldn't have this kid because both of her kids live with responsible adults

Caught my mom doing her daily drugs in the bathroom—she calls it her medicine, but I'm not that stupid, you don't snort your medicine

5 years

4 years

My father gets custody of me

My mom never shows up to court for me, bet she's too busy sniffing

I wish my father could have taken my brother too

Parents divorce when we are in Alaska but it isn't official until we move back to California

3 years
My mom is never around

2 years

1 year
When I was born I hated my mom
Every time she tried holding me I would cry; I believe that's how she got
  depressed.
I'd rather lie on my father's chest and have my father or brother feed me

Why We're Here

© Sylvia Sukop

(A few POPS kids have some words to say about the club …)

I came to POPS because I know what it's like to have a loved one in jail. I like being surrounded by people with the same problems as me. I feel like no one is alone. We all have someone to talk to. **Tanya Zarate**

I feel like I'm not alone. There are people who lost themselves, like me. I may not be friends or know them, but we're not alone. I may not have the same story they do, but I'm not alone. After all this time, throughout my depressed, thoughtful life, I actually found a place to stop keeping in my thoughts and just explode with my words. My past, I came here because my parents were constantly fighting, and I'm sorry that I can't fit in but…. **Tyanni Gomez**

I'm here because this is like my own personal counseling, and it helps me feel like the anger and pain I have in my life that I wish not to tell anybody about in person but on paper—that's another story, so they don't see me cry or get mad at something they think they understand but have no real connection to that situation. I just wanna be heard. I'm here to be myself, to say what I want to say and be. **Kei-Arri McGruder**

My dad served 20 years in state prison and that affected me a lot because he was not part of my childhood nor did I have contact with him. Many questions run through my head with no answers, and I need answers to be able to relax my mind. **Melissa Nava**

I came to POPS because I wanted to hear other peoples' stories. I don't want to be the only one going through so much pain. **Leslie Mateos**

I believe what brings me here is the absence of a father in my life. In many ways I can relate to those who in fact do have family members in prison. They have the gaping hole where someone they love, or ought to love, should be. They have all of the questions in the world to ask…. People would think that having a parent you know going to jail is one of the worst-case scenarios a child could have to go through—but what about those who never knew their father. **Angel Guerrero**

What brings me here today? I have to say food, and I haven't been in this room for a while now. I like to write. I consider myself good at it. I have stories to share, but I don't know…. **Krysten Robinson**

I am here because we are all a community and I love when presenters share their stories. My uncle was a heavy drug addict and is in and out of jail. He is out right now, and I want to know how to cope with seeing him like that. He still does drugs as well. I love the presentations. **Gabriel Bautista**

Portrait of Gabriel Bautista © Hannah Schatzle

I am not lost nor found
But I've come closer to knowing who I am
Getting caught up can change a lot
Even if all you're changing is just a thought

I'm here because I want to be.
Yeah, I got family locked up, but they ain't me.
Joslyn Stevenson

I am here for two things. One is to support my classmates/POPS members and two is for the food. I've had uncles in and out of jail for minor incidents. **Naelly Sernas**

I have an image of a month-long calendar with Xs in every day but big wide Os on all the Wednesdays (POPS days). **Leo Cruz**

I come to POPS because it makes me think of my dad. I feel closer to him in ways I can't describe when I come to POPS. When I'm here I can see him sitting in one of those seats. **Anonymous**

I come to POPS because I feel safe here in this room—it feels like I am not at school. I enjoy hearing my fellow classmates' stories, and I realized I was not the only one dealing with secrets or issues that are hard to express. P.S. I love POPS. **Marianne Valencia**

I come to POPS because my brother is in prison and I haven't seen him in six years. Just coming to POPS makes me feel that I'm not alone, and the only one who has someone who has been in jail/prison. I can say that being here is like home. I've improved throughout my time in POPS. **Bianca Lopez**

I am here because I like hearing the stories. I want to be a counselor, and this club gives me the opportunity to listen to what everyone goes through. I also like writing about things that go on in my life that are hard for me to say out loud. This club makes me feel safe. The image that comes to mind is a big family of students. **Ana Perez**

Lots of things bring me into this classroom—I love the environment, the people, and the wonderful food. I hope POPS turns into a bigger community to help people all over. **Anonymous**

Friends of POPS

Walking on Strands

by John Rodriguez

The fibers are twisted together in a braid and meant to hold the weight of 23 years of harsh memories. I hope it doesn't snap. My toes are cold with the pushing of the wind, but I would prove Momma right if I lose my balance. She always wanted me to fall. I have to hold on. I was never too good at symmetry, let alone measurements, but I have only about 17 feet to go. A tight rope and I ask myself what the f___ am I doing here? Walk a straight line for punishment. This is what it must feel like if I ever get pulled over for a DUI. Each step is another prayer, a moment to clear my consciousness and make amends before I plunge to my death. I wonder if it will hurt. Will I slip or hang on? Will my hands bulge with veins and help me find my strength or quiver in disgust and simply take a loss? Who tied the knots at either end and made sure they were secure? I look back and am ashamed at what I see, so I look ahead and try to progress. Life looks good on the other side, but it's maybe a lure to get me to conform to norms that are accepted by most. Should I let go? I know what's behind me, and it's something I don't want to relive. Tight rope, I'll just stay here for now until I figure it out because, here, it's just you and me. I'll hang on, but please don't make my hands bleed.

She's Tumbling

by John Rodriguez

Peace is a process. Peace within me while everything surrounding booms with cordite. Peace is losing. Peace is definitely not winning. Peace is bleeding on its side while the ambulance wails and its heart longs for a beat, its vessels for a pump, its lungs for a breath. Peace is slowly dying. Peace is unsure and weary. Peace has white blood cells rushing to her every wound. They're fighting to keep her alive, but no immune response will save this peace. Peace is stirred up, intoxicated off the morphine. Peace screams in her head, but I'm sorry, honey. Momma's not gonna hear you. Peace dances with devils in an elegant dress. Peace spilled red wine that seeped through her skin. She never knew how to waltz.

Doctors scream and jolt her purple skin with volts, compress air into her lungs, cut her up and try to paste her back together. Peace is getting sleepy. Sweet lullabies, loved ones wave goodbye. A little dirt on the lid to make it authentic. The light flickers out and doesn't burn continuously.

Hopefully she'll be resurrected.

I Don't Really Say Too Much

By John Bembry

You are the person you are and the one you choose to be. I'm my own person. But I don't really say too much.

I've been quiet almost all my life, making it through solo. Yeah, many people have played a good role supporting me. The person I am kept them around, not because I said Stay. I've lost too many people by relationships and death. I don't recall saying too much. Most things aren't my fault or I would man up and admit my flaws.

Expression is one of the key items that makes me a talented artist, but I don't really say too much. Unless you have a nice beat.

I talked about being detained and systematized. I don't really say too much about it now. That a long leap of time is done and behind me. Did I learn? Did I grow? You tell me.

POPS, from the day I first began coming out of a hole in a seat to now planning my same dreams with more ambition, growing education and a painful past to learn from. I don't like to say too much.

I've been doubted severely, so I would love to show people differently. The scholarship could help me do a lot of things. I would invest in my clothing designs and collaborations with other business people. I could help POPS and pay back Amy and Annie, finally, even though all they ask in return is that I keep writing.

I don't know how far I would go because my passion in writing comes with a nice rhythm. Yet I doubt that I won't be successful. I don't say too much about myself when asked, "What will you be when you grow up?" Only the dream I believe in. Supporters are fans, and they help my dreams happen.

I can't thank every one of them enough.

After everything I've endured, I pray to and thank God I haven't perished from this earth.

So many tears have been shed, hearts broken, blood spilled, and dreams crushed. I mysteriously was able to survive and speak about it.

That is why I need an education. If you have friends, make sure they're the right ones to be around. There's nothing wrong with being alone. My heart is rock solid thanks to relationships and more.

Devastating times those were, but with all the knowledge I have acquired over time, with all the help from POPS and other real people I know, I've survived. I couldn't be more grateful things aren't worse.

I have a bright future ahead of me. I know I must stay focused and give all my effort. I know life is unfair, but it's somewhat tolerable. I know very much I don't speak of. I don't really say too much.

You are the person you are and the one you choose to be. I am my own person. And I don't really say too much.

Breaking the Cycle

by Michael A. Davis

POPS the Club came to my attention during a recent conversation with a fellow convict named Boston Woodard. After being told what POPS the Club was all about, I felt compelled to offer my input and perspective in regard to "the pain of the prison system" and how it relates to me.

It's sadly astounding the profound impact that having a parent in prison can have on a child. The invariable feelings of misplaced guilt and blame, the never-ending uncertainty, the lack of having a proper traditional family structure, along with the shame and embarrassment that comes with having a parent in prison, can take a heavy psychological and emotional toll on a child who doesn't know how to appropriately express their feelings and thoughts.

Regrettably, more times than not the negative results can be far reaching and have lifelong side effects. The ripple effect can go on for generations, and I assure you that that ripple effect can be directly linked to a lot of the dysfunction going on in society today. Growing up with a parent in prison is a painful dilemma no child should be saddled with, but unfortunately in today's society, it's a reoccurring reality for too many children.

I am intimately familiar with this particular subject because I am the child of a parent who was in prison for a large part of my life. I am also the parent of a child who was forced to endure having a parent in prison for his entire life. And now my son just so happens to be an incarcerated parent of a child who has been forced to endure growing up with a parent in prison. Like I said, the cycle can go on for generations.

In short, this is my story...

Growing up in the 1970s, the only interaction I remember having with my biological father was through the periodic phone calls or once-in-a-blue-moon letters he'd write that I'd get while visiting my grandmother over the summer. My father passed away in 2010 due to complications related to diabetes, and the one lasting impression I have of him is that he was never there for me, ever. I grew up blaming him for everything bad that ever happened to me (misplaced blame). My blame was unfair, but it was the reasoning I used in my decision-making process with so many of the poor choices I made in my younger years growing up in an unstructured environment. I vowed to be nothing like my father, but ironically, I ended up being exactly like my father!

One day, when it truly dawned on me how messed up my circumstances actually were, I determined to change them. I decided that I would be the one to initiate breaking the cycle of incarceration that literally has plagued my family for generations! I reached out to my incarcerated son and shared with him my desire to change our circumstances, and he too devoted himself to breaking the cycle. By the time you're reading this piece, my son will have been released from prison after doing 4½ years, and I have high hopes that he and I together will break the cycle!

I changed the condition of my heart and became the author of *Deeply Rooted* in 2012. I also mentor at-risk youth here at the prison where I'm incarcerated. My son converted to Islam, and he too changed the condition of his heart and aspires to be great in his lifetime.

While our stories didn't start out well, they most definitely have taken a turn for the better, and my son and I are as resolute as ever to follow through with breaking this appalling generational curse of "parenting while in prison' that has inundated our family for generations.

Programs like POPS the Club are essential in helping families break the cycle and heal from and/or deal with the pain of having a loved one in prison, so they will always have my undying support!!! Thank you to all the hard-working people at POPS the Club.

The Original POPS Kid

by Boston Woodard

Two years ago I learned about POPS the Club from author/poet Judith Tannenbaum. "It's a great program for young students who have a parent or loved one in prison through no fault of their own," she said. After pondering her words, it occurred to me that no one really talks much about the wounding effect prison has on all those kids left behind when a loved one is imprisoned. It's as if they did not exist. They are real. The voids in their lives are huge, and at times extremely painful.

Judith felt having something written about POPS the Club by a prisoner would be important as we live the life we write about. I thought it was a great idea and agreed with her about how important POPS the Club is. The more I learned about the group, the clearer it became that this may be one of the most important new prisoner-related programs to come down the pike in decades. I could not wait to write an article about POPS the Club.

After several communications with POPS the Club co-founder Amy Friedman, I had the background information I needed for my article. As I learned more about the club, the more drawn into its purpose I became. Although my tumultuous upbringing was not a direct result of a particular prison association, it had everything to do with the absence of a parent, my father, in my life from a very young age.

In the early 1960s, my father abandoned my mother with five kids when I was eight years old. I never wanted to talk about him or what he had done to our family. I have no recollection of our father hitting or beating us kids, but I do remember him hitting my mother on numerous occasions. The memory of my father hitting my mother has crowded my brain for many decades—it never goes away. I'm a firm believer now that talking about my father's behavior then is important. Talking about it helps me to understand how anger can take control of someone and ruin their life, and the lives of others, for many years to come if not addressed.

My grandparents (on my mother's side of the family) raised my older brother Ron after our father ran off. My three sisters—Georgine, Jane, and Lori—and I remained with our mother. I was pretty much raised on the streets, ignoring everything good my mother was trying to instill in me. I had no father figure in my life. I was a POPS kids before there was a POPS the Club.

When I came to prison I had a beautiful wife and an infant son I never got to know. Forty years later, I have never met him. It's a hole in my heart I can never heal. My wife divorced me not long after my incarceration. She remarried, and I never heard from her or my son again. I take full responsibility regarding my son and the reason he is not in my life today. Just like all great POPS kids, my son was only guilty of having a father in prison who did some bad things. I can only pray he is happy today.

Occasionally my mother would try to discipline me—to no avail. At the age of ten, the year President John F. Kennedy was assassinated, I was in the fifth grade. Two years later, I somehow made it to the seventh grade, and that was the extent of my education on the outside. I could barely read, and my writing was probably around third-grade level. I took it upon myself to self-educate. The streets were my classroom and experienced criminals were my teachers. Had there been a POPS the Club in my life during that time, it's highly likely life would have served me a different outcome.

With my mother, Barbara, on welfare trying to keep us fed, attempting to make ends meet, and without any real parental oversight of my daily activities, I took advantage and began doing whatever I wished. I knew nothing about the Boy Scouts of America, the Y.M.C.A., Boys Clubs, or any other groups and events many young kids are exposed to. I can only imagine what life would be like today had I been exposed to something as important as POPS the Club. The program would have been positive incentive for me to remain in school and develop important self-esteem and social skills all young people deserve.

I read *Runaway Thoughts,* the POPS the Club's first anthology, and I was absolutely blown away by the talent expressed in the book. Page after page, I could relate to so much of what I read. POPS the Club members reached way down into their souls to produce that level of honesty. What impressed me most were the young writers' and artists' individual expressions of their sometimes painful realities. Unbelievably candid! They should be proud of themselves for their accomplishment.

What POPS the Club co-founders Amy Friedman, Dennis Danziger, and Anastasia Stanecki have set in motion is what I believe to be an educational experience of a lifetime. Young people in schools all over the country whose lives have been adversely altered due to the pain of the prison system should have access to such a wonderful family as is POPS the Club.

I have committed to stepping up to lend a hand with what support I am able to offer this amazing concept called POPS the Club.

Two Left Feet

by Robin Ledbetter

I'm a member of a group almost obsolete
A Black girl with two left feet
I can't dance.
But it's okay…because I strut to my own beat.
You may see me occasionally gliding from here to there
oblivious to what's around me, seemingly unaware
but my slow drag is what they call sa…voir…faire
Tactful sophistication in an oppressing situation
I have music playing in my own head
And as I step with these legs made out of lead
I sway to the alluring music, pulling me, homestead.
Homeward bound
No matter how many times I get kicked to the ground
I pull myself up enticed by that sound
Homeward bound
This place can have everything, except the individualism I wear as a crown
Because I'm a queen
A queen with two left feet
But I'll walk and I'll run and I'll dance to the rhythm of my beat
Dance and dance and dance till *these* touch the street
They've shackled my hands and feet
Given me a number to strip me of my identity
Or at least, they tried…but they don't know I'm not the norm
So they can keep trying to force me to conform
Blurring my image with this anonymous burgundy and blue uniform
But I'm me, always me, and I'll never bleed into the walls of this facility
I can stay in this motherfucker for an eternity and I'll still shake it to my own beat
Dance, dance the dance of the free with these sore-ass two left feet…and be me
Robin…also known as unique!

What I Want to Say

by Robin Ledbetter

What I want to say is to the faith pushers,
The Jesus *prais'ers*,
The Christian *enslavers*.

Those who tell me to give it to God,
I want to talk to you about faith.

This is for those of us who once had *faith*,
Who got it kicked and beat out of them,
Who left it on bloodied sheets after *rape*.

I believe, I *praised*,
Took Communion, got *saved*.

But god left me …
Abandoned me …
Had me fend for *myself*,
So I lost my faith …
Retired …
Put it up on the *shelf*

Young girl beaten, left battered and *broken*
Cried rivers on my knees
Marooned in hell, left *soak'en*

So I prayed …
Now I lay me down to sleep
I pray dear Lord I won't get beat
Just let me die before I wake
I pray dear Lord let me escape …

And then I'd wake.
I *always* went to him in prayer.

Getting my ass whooped I *cried,*
"Please God, **Save Me! Save Me!**
I'm Dying *Inside!"*

While he invaded my body I said a silent *prayer*
"Please God, he's hurting me.
Are you listening?
Are you *there?"*

They say all it takes is faith the size of a mustard *seed,*
But after a greenhouse full of faith, I let the devil take the
    lead.

Once you make friends with the Devil
And shake hands in a *pact*
You exchange your soul for a small price,
and you can never get it *back*

So I prayed…
        To the fallen angel Lucifer I offer up my soul,
          All I want in exchange is a little control.
            Give me the strength to fight back,
              the strength to be free,
               No longer a victim,
               the strength to be me.

Now …
I sit in my *cell,*
My own personal *hell,*

And ponder this thing called faith.

And as my insides *decay*
And I can't see past *today*
This is what I want to *say…*

To the faith pushers,
The Jesus *prais'ers,*
The Christian *enslavers,*

    CAN GOD REALLY SAVE US?

Where I'm From

by Robin Ledbetter

I'm from brick buildings and concrete parks.
From the place where old Hispanic men work on car
    engines all day while drinking Budweiser
And slick-talking, chain-smoking old women hang both
    themselves and their clothes out the window.
I'm from Pit bulls and Rottweilers, from hoodies and
               Tims,
Where Vienna sausages, Hog head cheese, and Oodles
    of noodles are considered a meal.
   I'm from a place where a bride can wear black, the
Groom a top hat and cane, and a reception consists of
       40 drinking and weed smoke.
I'm from weed smoke, crack smoke, coke heads, dope
    heads, base heads, and no basements.
        I'm from laughter.
From BBQ's with three generations.
        Dominos, spades
And Auntie Robin's drunken dance requesting
Lisa Stanfield's "Been Around the World" for the
      Twelfth time.
I'm from games like red light/green light, knock-knock
      Zum-zum,
   And "Can you keep a secret" with grown folks.
     I'm from secrets.
  I'm from curry powder and baby powder
  From hair grease and bacon grease
      I'm from RedHot hot sauce.
I'm from a place where we keep the dead alive with
      Spray-painted murals,
Graffiti-tagged tees and tapping a bottle then spilling
    the liquid.
I'm from chunky jewelry, rap music, bike handles,
coconut icies, penny candies and quarter snacks.
I'm from "You better be home before the streetlights
    come on!"

I'm from roaches that lie face-up, drowned in a puddle
of Raid.
Where down South is the motherland.
I'm from government cheese, powdered milk,
And buying a day's worth of groceries.
Grandma carrying a Bible she cannot read
Daddy missing
Mommy's love a memory.
I'm from cradling my pillow every night in place of my
little sister.
I'm from a place of longing.
I'm from brick buildings and concrete parks.
I'm from the hood.

Letter to My Sister

by Jordan Lopez

What up, Dumbo! Thanx for the X-mas card. I hope all of you have a great time. I wish I could have spent these holidays with all of you, but it's the same thing every year for me. When these days come around is when I think of the family the most. But in here it feels like any other day because nothing special goes on. Same shit, different smell. Another day gone by. I'm doing all right, always remaining optimistic with my chin held high. Posted like a chess piece and thinking before I take my next move. Because life gets pivotal in the middle game.

I was surprised by your poem. You made me remember how bad a brother I've been. I could only imagine how my absence has affected you, and I know there are NO words to explain how sorry I am for not being around, but believe it or not, I wish I could go back and change things. Life was too quick for me, and instead of being decisive with my choices and getting off on the right exit, I kept going down the same road and ended up in a life-long dead end of a cell. And for that reason I ALWAYS say, be good and take care of Mom. I've put her through enough. Also, I ask you to make correct choices throughout your life. There are going to be times when you're gonna have to think quick and you're gonna feel the pressure, thinking the odds are against you, but reality is, your intuition conquers all. Always feel confident in handling a situation. Don't ever feel like a bug—easy to be squashed. Lift your head up and let your mind flow like a river. Remain poised at all times. Well, my little sis, "Dumbo," by next month, "Big Dumbo!" You've done grown up on me. It's true what they say, "Time flies!" I wish things were different, but life isn't perfect for anyone. Life is cruel, but cruelest to the weak. Even though I'm far away, locked in a cell, I'm easy to reach. Please don't let these walls stop our blood flow. I love you!

Well, Bianca, just so you know, I have stopped drawing and started focusing on books. So I'm sorry if I don't send you a drawing for your book, but I do write poetry. So here's one I did not long ago.

The River Without Water

A haggard Man sits and awaits.
Under a shadow & no wind to feel.
Bones have become transparent to skin.
Lack of energy to speak the knowledge he knows.
Whispers of wisdom. Does it enter your ear?
I wish for an echo, but it never appears.
Arises and falls, so he sits and awaits
             Under a shadow.
No one looks! No one cares!
Who would dare exchange places and emaciate?
DON'T BE A FOOL AND CONSIDER!
I am the sacrifice because it
Shouldn't have, if it wasn't meant for me.
Under a shadow. I sit and await.
My time will come
To finally smile.

All right now, Lil Sis, I love you. Until next time.

Advice to
Ninth-Graders

Don't let your so-called friends drag you down with them. —**Marianne Valencia**

You'll be cooler than the "cool kids" if you pay half the attention in class as they do at parties. —**De'Jon K. Jones**

Keep your focus on yourself and your goals. Many people make the mistake of letting their relationships get in the way of their education. Just think, what will these people do for you in 10 years when you're trying to pay your rent? —**Maya Iwata**

If there is something you don't like, stand up and change it yourself.— **Anonymous**

Be friendly and talk to as many people as possible. —**Anonymous**

Your middle school friends will disappear. —**Anonymous**

There are a lot of dumb boys; be smart about who you meet. —**Kat Secaida**

Smoke outside of school, not inside. —**Andrew Hernandez**

© Eduardo Hernandez

Author Bios

Gabriel Bautista is a Venice High student who has high goals and aspirations for the future.

Melanie Becerra is a senior who dreams of becoming a professional musician.

Ia'Leah Cain believes in being nobody but herself in this world and by doing that does her best, night and day.

Jeannie Cajas is an 18-year-old senior who is passionate about music; marching band, choir, and guitar give her the therapy to get by.

Randy Chavez is a young kid with big dreams but is getting screwed by going to Mexico.

Anthony Cortez is a man of few words. He comes from many places and has overcome many obstacles. He is heading nowhere in particular.

Leo Cruz is a senior at Venice High and an avid San Francisco 49er fan.

Kemontae Dafney is a student athlete who was raised by sports. Any sport you name he can play and is good at it.

Angel De La Cruz chooses his own destiny.

Elia Guadalupe Espinosa is a 17-year-old girl ready for what life has to offer, and future U.S. president.

Luis A. Fajardo is a youngun', calls himself the Captain of the Space Ship. He has no destination and is never coming down.

Erika Fernandez is a VHS senior who loves to spend time with friends and family and plans to attend college.

Tyanni Gomez is just a 17-year-old girl who loves writing, hoping it will mean something to someone one day.

Angel Guerrero is a 17-year-old junior at Venice High School, living in Los Angeles, California, and a real cool guy!

Irvin Gutierrez-Lopez will graduate from VHS in June. He went from dreaming of becoming a gangster to dreaming of becoming a screenwriter and director.

Alberto Hernandez is a VHS senior who likes to hustle and surf the waves at Venice Beach. He plans on studying law enforcement after graduation.

Andrew Hernandez is a sophomore who will continue on his high school career and hopes to pursue all his dreams.

Mariana Hernandez is a student sitting in Mr. Danziger's class who started with picking up a pen, and now I'm a writer.

Maya Iwata is a senior at Venice High, born and raised in Los Angeles, California. She is taking life day by day, waiting to see where the wind will take her.

Grecia Jara is a 17-year-old struggling in life like any other. Special love and thanks to A.J. Duffy for helping me express my feelings, find myself, and write my story.

De'Jon K. Jones is a nobody with an imagination amongst a lot of somebodies. Foreseen star. Ignorance is bliss.

Zaria Lampkins. I love POPS. If this could be a class, I'd probably get an A in it.

Nichole Landaverde finds peace in writing.

D. Leigh is a senior at Venice High School who enjoys swimming and media arts and plans to become an orthopedic surgeon.

Bianca Lopez is a senior at Venice High School who loves food and is visiting her brother!

Daisy Lopez is a very happy young lady, smart, good cook, wants to study to be a chef, likes to party and have others laugh.

Dannie Maddox is a girl who lives in a big world with big dreams with a small heart and a little bit of inspiration.

Alondra Magallanes is a Venice High senior and an inaugural member of POPS the Club.

Nelvia Marin is a Venice High senior ready for a four-year college.

Leslie Mateos is a 19-year-old Venice High School senior. She is an only child who lives with her mom who feels like she's gone through a lot in her short life.

Kei-Arri McGruder is a 16-year-old visual writer who plays sports and has a bright future ahead of her.

Michelle Montano no longer attends Venice High School but continues to write about her life.

J. Murray. Yonkers. Harlem World. Murray Hill. Empire. Young Picasso. You feel me? I thought so. Love be to rap what key be to lock.

Melissa L. Nava is Mexican-American and proud to be the daughter of an amazing mother/father, Virginia R. Flores.

Ana Perez is a student at Venice High School who won't let anyone or anything stop her from achieving her goals.

Chelsea Ramseur is a senior with dreams of becoming an English teacher, with hopes of spreading the love I have for writing.

Michaela Richards believes POPS the Club is a positive outlet for students who carry the pain of the prison system on our shoulders every day—whether prison has impacted our lives directly or the lives of the people we love. POPS gives us all a place to come together where we can be understood.

Anthony Manuel Rios. You will never know me until you walk in my shoes.

Krystan Robinson is a junior at Venice High who likes martial arts and would like to have a career in that discipline.

Alejandra Ruiz is a senior at Venice High who loves spending time with animals more than with people.

Jaquelin Sanchez is a high school senior who loves spending time with friends and having fun.

Kat Secaida is a small girl in a big world, a young tenth-grader learning how to release anger through writing.

Naelly Sernas is a senior at Venice High who loves reading and softball.

Qahirah (Q) Smith is a VHS senior moving to Georgia to attend University of West Georgia and is going for a doctoral degree in clinical psychology.

Joslyn Stevenson. I am who I am because I'm understanding and open-minded.

Marianne Valencia will not let my past negatively affect me.

Miguel Gianfranco Guzman Valle is a Venice High School student who has come to another country to face and struggle with English and enjoys working with computers.

Veronica Vargas is a senior at Venice High School who only hopes to make something of herself and prove everyone wrong who said she'd fail.

Chelina Vasquez is a Venice High School senior, POPS vice president, and she loves cheese.

Julissa L. Vega is just another teenager making it through school and life.

Angelee Velasquez loves spending time with her sisters and going out with her friends. She loves chocolate ice cream and watching Netflix.

Brittany Weight believes that "People's perception of you is their reality."

Tanya Zarate is a senior at Venice High waiting eagerly for graduation day and is finally going to enter the real world where she plans to study for a tech career in ultrasound or dentistry.

Portrait of Alonda Magallanes © Hannah Schatzle

Portrait of Chelina Vasquez © Hannah Schatzle

Friends of POPS Bios

John Bembry graduated from Venice High in 2014 and remains a loyal POPS "kid." John makes music!

Michael A. Davis To learn more about Michael visit Facebook@IceMike the Author or follow him on Instagram & Twitter @IceMikeWritenow! THE SKY IS THE LIMIT!

Victor L.M. Demic whose artwork graces these covers is a 2014 graduate of Venice High. Victor continues to produce beautiful paintings and photography and to hone his craft.

Eduardo Hernandez graduated from Venice High in 2014 and remains a faithful POPS friend. His photography helps to illustrate our world.

Robin Ledbetter is a friend of POPS the club who knows the gift of writing and friendship. Robin is serving a 50-year sentence in prison, a sentence she received when she was 14 years old. You can read more about Robin in her award-winning PEN America Free Expression story: www.pen.org/nonfiction-essay/laying-roots.

John Rodriguez is a longtime friend of POPS co-founders who continues to write prolifically. John also teaches creative writing.

Boston Woodard is a prisoner/freelance journalist, author of *Inside the Broken California Prison System* and co-author with prisoners' rights advocate and journalist Maria Telesco of the soon-to-be released *PRISON: The Ins and Outs.* Boston says, "I'm a POPS kid before there was a POPS."

*"We tell ourselves stories
in order to live."*

-- Joan Didion